On a cold, damp afternoon in July 1939, at the Royal Naval College, Dartmouth, the 13-year-old Princess Elizabeth spotted a handsome – and penniless – young prince for the first time. Eight years later, Buckingham Palace proudly announced their engagement.

As Queen of England, with Prince Philip at her side, a unique partnership has blossomed into a deep and abiding love that has captured the hearts of her subjects for over 40 years.

ILN Picture Library

THE HAND OF FATE

FOR THE ENCHANTING PRINCESS ELIZABETH, HISTORY BECKONED EARLY. HEIR TO THE THRONE AT 13, SHE SOON MET AND SET HER SIGHTS ON THE DASHING NAVAL CADET, PHILIP MOUNTBATTEN OF GREECE

I N THE EARLY HOURS OF 21 April 1926, a miserable drizzle was falling outside 17 Bruton Street in London's Mayfair. Inside, after a troublesome pregnancy, the Duchess of York gave birth to a daughter by Caesarian section (officially described as 'a certain line of treatment'). The Palace announcement of the birth of the future Queen Elizabeth II ran as follows:

'Her Royal Highness the Duchess of York was safely delivered of a Princess at 2.40 am this morning, Wednesday, April 21st.'

The Duke had been worried to distraction during the final, difficult days of the Duchess's pregnancy, and it was a great relief to him when he finally gazed on his daughter.

As the Duke doted on his first-born, it never dawned on him that the little Princess would one day be Queen. For the moment, the greatest responsibility for the Yorks was choosing a name for the baby – always an exercise in tact and diplomacy within the Royal circle. Elizabeth was chosen to honour her mother. Two other names were added – Alexandra, after her Royal great-grandmother, and Mary after her grandmother.

At the time of her birth, Princess Elizabeth was third in line to the throne, following her own father, the Duke of York, and Edward, Prince of Wales (known in the family as David). To the press, it was just conceivable that she might one day inherit the throne, but this presupposed

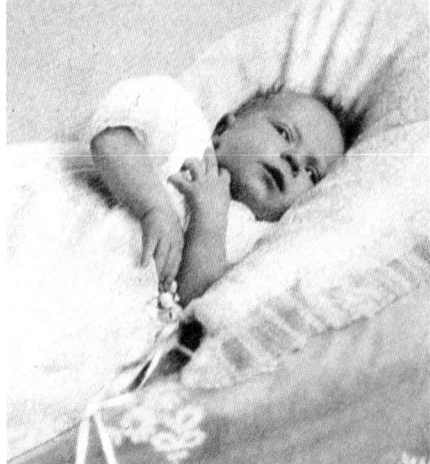

Rex Features

'It almost frightens me that the people should love her so much'

THE QUEEN MOTHER

that Edward would not marry, and also that her parents would not have sons to take precedence over her. *The Times* took the line that they would rather have been celebrating the engagement of the Prince of Wales than rejoicing over the Yorks' little girl.

Elizabeth spent much of her second year without her parents, whom George V sent on a six-month tour of the Empire.

With the Yorks on the other side of the world, George and Mary doted on their enchanting little granddaughter. They were very much more demonstrative than they had been with their own children. Queen Mary had never allowed her emotions to come between her and her almost mystical reverence for the Crown. Of her children, she frequently said: 'I never forget that their father is also their King.' But the Queen was delighted to take charge of the 'bambina', as she called the infant Elizabeth.

Princess Elizabeth was a good child, who observed the world with a steady, untroubled gaze. She was physically advanced, having four teeth at the age of 11 months, and swiftly learned to crawl, walk and utter simple words.

When their marathon tour ended, the Yorks could see for themselves the progress their daughter had made. On 27 June 1927, they proudly carried her out on to the balcony at Buckingham Palace before sinking with

♛ *You don't know what a tremendous joy it is to Elizabeth and me to have our little girl,' wrote the Duke of York to his mother. The birthplace of the future Queen Elizabeth II, 17 Bruton Street, Mayfair, was the London residence of her maternal grandparents, the Earl and Countess of Strathmore*

Marcus Adams/Camera Press

Hulton-Deutsch Collection

relief into a domestic routine in their new home at 145 Piccadilly.

Everyone adored the Yorks' little girl. When the Duke and Duchess returned from their tour they brought with them no less than three tons of toys and gifts for Elizabeth, and when she was three she was on the cover of *Time* magazine. Such adulation frankly worried her mother, who wrote to Queen Mary: 'It almost frightens me that the people should love her so much. I suppose that is a good thing, and I hope she will be worthy of it, poor little darling.'

Idyllic life

The arrival of a sister stole some of the limelight away from Elizabeth. Princess Margaret Rose was born at Glamis Castle on 21 August 1930. Her birth had been so difficult that it seemed likely that there was no possibility of any more York children.

The two Princesses led an idyllic life at 145 Piccadilly. Unlike most other privileged children of the day, they had no single fixed hour at which, freshly bathed and dressed, they were to be presented to their parents. The Yorks were remarkably modern, allowing the little girls to explore every room. Bathtime was always hilarious and resulted in regular drenchings for 'Us Four', as the Duke referred to his family.

Elizabeth, who had been given her first pony, Peggy, when she was only three, was already obsessed with all things equestrian. By contrast, Margaret was the comedian of the family. Even as a toddler she was funny, with an

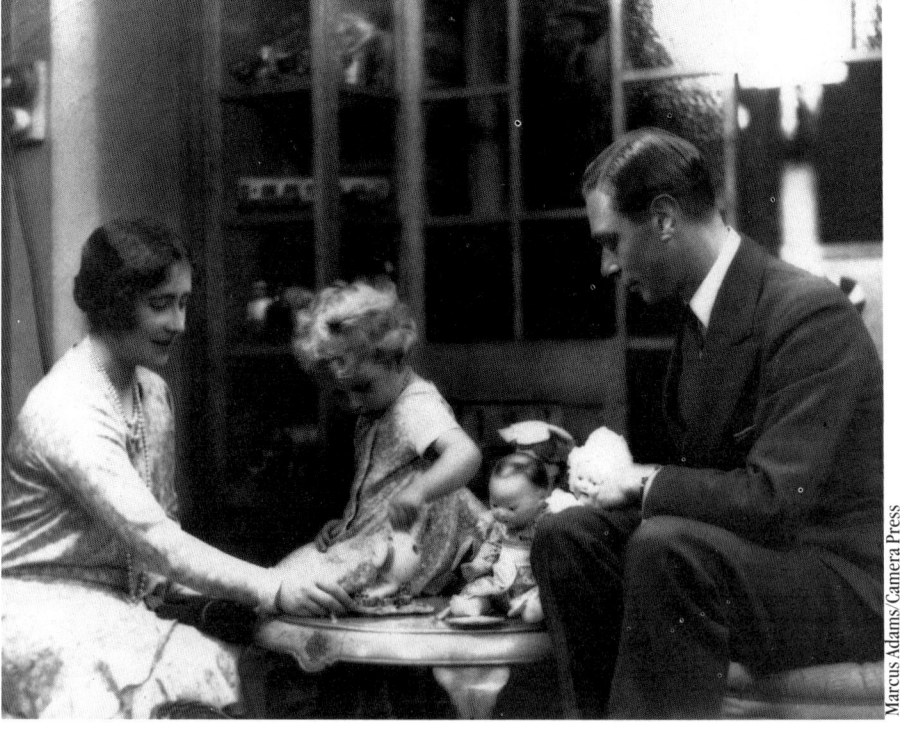

Marcus Adams/Camera Press

impeccable sense of timing. 'You can forgive her anything, she is so amusing,' said Queen Mary.

In 1931, the Duke and Duchess of York took over Royal Lodge in Windsor Great Park, with its separate Little House, more properly called *Y Bwthyn Bach*, as playhouse for the Princesses – a gift to them from the people of Wales.

While Margaret could be something of a handful, Elizabeth's only known act of rebellion was characteristically aimed at herself. Driven wild by the vagaries of irregular French verbs, she once poured the contents of an

♛ *A joy to her parents, the little Princess was also taken to heart by the British people who were even persuaded to buy chocolates bearing her picture* below

Robert Opie

ROYAL GUARDIANS

The growing 'Lilibet', as she called herself, was entrusted to the care of three influential women. Nurse Clara Knight *right* was known as 'Allah', after Elizabeth's earliest attempts to pronounce her name. Governess Marion Crawford ('Crawfie') and Margaret 'Bobo' MacDonald – who to this day remains dresser and personal friend to the Queen – are pictured *far right* with their young charge and a friend at London Zoo. Crawfie was a tall, straightbacked young woman with very definite ideas on how to bring up young ladies, even if they were Princesses

Hulton-Deutsch Collection

inkpot over her own head. Margaret grew to be philosophical about being ticked off and even developed a mythical 'Cousin Halifax' who, she declared, was responsible for her various misdemeanours.

Their governess, Marion Crawford ('Crawfie') took them on rather daring trips into the outside world. Once they even went unnoticed on the London Underground to Tottenham Court Road and had tea at the YWCA. When Elizabeth was told off by the tea lady for leaving her teapot somewhere inconvenient, the little party was recognized and a royal car was hastily summoned. On another occasion, they sat on the top deck of a bus, much amused to be able to look into other people's back gardens. At Queen Mary's insistence, they also visited art galleries and museums – the Queen was most concerned that they should grow up with a proper appreciation of art.

First meeting

In 1934 Elizabeth was one of the bridesmaids at the wedding of the Duke of Kent (Uncle George) and the beautiful Princess Marina of Greece. Also present at the celebrations was a certain Philip of Greece, although neither was to remember meeting the other at this event.

When George V celebrated his Silver Jubilee in 1935 with a Thanksgiving Service at St Paul's Cathedral, Elizabeth and Margaret were dressed identically in pink coats and pink hats decorated with pink petals. Time was running out for the King. Eight years earlier, he had been so gravely ill that rumours flew thick and fast that he was dying. Now, his beloved sister Victoria died a couple of weeks before Christmas 1935, and after struggling through the Sandringham festivities the King himself died on 20 January 1936. The Crown now passed to Edward VIII.

The Princesses were taking tea with their parents in the Royal Lodge early in 1936 when the new King arrived to show them his American station wagon – and, in it, an American friend, Mrs Ernest Simpson. Later, as Duchess of Windsor, Mrs Simpson recalled the polite, meticulously dressed York girls – and the coolness with which their mother greeted her.

While stormclouds were gathering for the new King, the future Queen and her younger sister continued with their schoolwork and enjoyed riding, exercising the dogs, picnicking, Girl Guide activities (today Princess Margaret is President of the Guides' Association), swimming and dancing lessons. A governess exclaimed that 'Margaret Rose may be quicksilver but Elizabeth is pure gold.'

In December 1936, Marion Crawford was hurrying her elder charge into a car when Elizabeth caught sight of a placard that read:

👑 *Elizabeth's love of dogs and horses was evident early on. In 1937, the Coronation of her father as George VI made her the heir presumptive to the throne. As she stood outside Buckingham Palace* left, *her carefree childhood was effectively over*

'King to decide tonight.' She turned to her governess with an earnest question: 'Is Uncle David in trouble?'

Edward VIII had taken the agonizing decision to abdicate, and on 10 December his short reign was over. Seeing an envelope on the hall table addressed to 'HM The Queen' Elizabeth said: 'That's Mummy now, isn't it?'

Margaret asked, 'Does that mean that you will have to be Queen one day?'

'Yes, some day,' replied Elizabeth.

'Poor you,' said Margaret.

Heir presumptive

Elizabeth's idyllic childhood was over. When George VI was crowned King on 12 May 1937, his elder daughter and heir, though she had barely turned 11, had already begun the lonely and arduous training for the role of Queen.

Among the glittering throng of Coronation guests was the dashing young Prince Philip of Greece. But it was two more years before Elizabeth met her future husband.

That meeting took place in 1939 at Dartmouth Naval College, which Elizabeth and Margaret were visiting at the invitation of their uncle, Lord 'Dickie' Mountbatten. Prince Philip, a new college recruit, was deputed to entertain the young Princesses. A nephew of Mountbatten, he shared his uncle's attractively arrogant swagger (but not, at this stage, the Mountbatten name, which he adopted later).

The young Philip

Although Elizabeth and Philip were related by blood, their backgrounds were only superficially similar. The fact was that Prince Philip of Greece had not a drop of real Greek blood in his veins. In 1863, when a proud new Greek nation emerged from an epic struggle against Turkey, Philip's grandfather – then a Danish prince – had accepted an invitation to establish a Greek royal family by becoming the country's first King, George I.

Prince Philip was thus a direct descendant of the first Danish-Greek Royal Family. He was born in a villa on Corfu, on 10 June 1921. The short history of the new Greek mon-

♛ **The nine-year-old Philip of Greece wearing the national dress of his family's adoptive country**

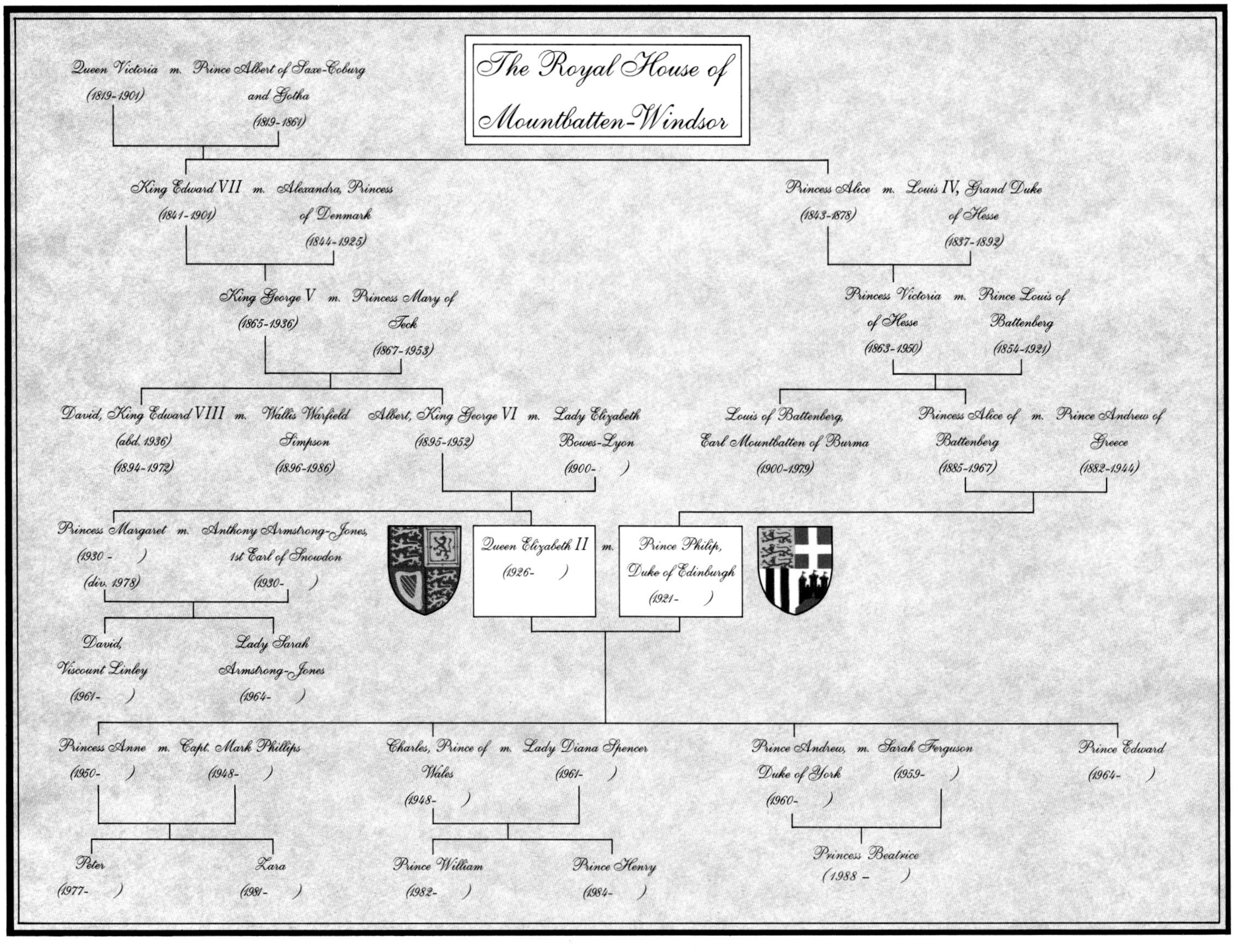

The Royal House of Mountbatten-Windsor

Queen Victoria m. Prince Albert of Saxe-Coburg and Gotha
(1819-1901) (1819-1861)

King Edward VII m. Alexandra, Princess of Denmark
(1841-1901) (1844-1925)

Princess Alice m. Louis IV, Grand Duke of Hesse
(1843-1878) (1837-1892)

King George V m. Princess Mary of Teck
(1865-1936) (1867-1953)

Princess Victoria of Hesse m. Prince Louis of Battenberg
(1863-1950) (1854-1921)

David, King Edward VIII m. Wallis Warfield Simpson
(abd. 1936) (1896-1986)
(1894-1972)

Albert, King George VI m. Lady Elizabeth Bowes-Lyon
(1895-1952) (1900-)

Louis of Battenberg, Earl Mountbatten of Burma
(1900-1979)

Princess Alice of Battenberg m. Prince Andrew of Greece
(1885-1967) (1882-1944)

Princess Margaret m. Anthony Armstrong-Jones, 1st Earl of Snowdon
(1930-) (1930-)
(div. 1978)

Queen Elizabeth II m. Prince Philip, Duke of Edinburgh
(1926-) (1921-)

David, Viscount Linley (1961-)

Lady Sarah Armstrong-Jones (1964-)

Princess Anne m. Capt. Mark Phillips
(1950-) (1948-)

Charles, Prince of Wales m. Lady Diana Spencer
(1948-) (1961-)

Prince Andrew, Duke of York m. Sarah Ferguson
(1960-) (1959-)

Prince Edward (1964-)

Peter (1977-)

Zara (1981-)

Prince William (1982-)

Prince Henry (1984-)

Princess Beatrice (1988-)

archy had already been blighted by assassinations, abdications and exile, and Philip was only a year old when his family were forced to leave the island hurriedly aboard a British cruiser put at their disposal on the orders of George V. There was no time to make a dignified exit – Philip began his new life in a carrycot made from orange boxes.

By the time Philip was born, his parents' marriage was at an end. Prince Andrew of Greece and Princess Alice of Battenberg (Lord Mountbatten's sister) already had four daughters a good deal older than their son. The couple's interests were completely divergent. She was intensely religious and in future years would found an order of nuns in Greece. Prince Andrew was an impecunious but charming playboy. It was inevitable that the two should part company.

High spirits

But who would bring up young Philip? Princess Alice (or 'Princess Andrew' as she was more properly known) sought the help of her brothers, George, Marquess of Milford Haven and Louis ('Dickie') Mountbatten. At first, Philip grew up with both his parents in the shabby-genteel world of the disinherited aristocrat in Paris, where he attended the American School (and acquired an American accent). But after his parents' final separation, Uncle George took Philip under his wing, sending him to Cheam Preparatory School.

Philip's behaviour was high-spirited at school and often outrageous at home. Partly to counter this rebellious streak, in 1933 Uncle George sent Philip to the Salem School, close to the Bavarian border, in Germany. Philip's sister Theodora, who lived nearby in Schloss Salem, kept an eye on her younger brother.

Even in 1933 the sinister influence of the Nazi youth movement was creeping into every institution in Germany. Salem School had been founded on the highest principles of a 'healthy

☙ *Philip's father* inset *was a penniless aristocrat. Philip himself was a rather impetuous child. The athletic rigours of Gordonstoun quickly matured him*

☙ *At 13, Elizabeth* front row *saw the 18-year-old naval cadet Philip of Greece* standing, far right *at Dartmouth Naval College for the first time*

mind in a healthy body' by the great educationalist Kurt Hahn, but his courageous stand against Nazism landed him in prison. Significantly, during these years, the young Philip – who would later be attacked repeatedly by the media for insensitivity – made a point of giving his own school cap to a Jewish boy whose head had been shaved. When, thanks to some behind-the-scenes diplomacy by the British Government, Hahn gained his release, he went to Scotland to set about building his ideal school from scratch. It was called Gordonstoun House and one of its first pupils was Philip of Greece.

An exuberant, inflexible teenager, Philip tended to storm through life. Kurt Hahn, his great hero, made these telling comments in his final school report: 'Prince Philip is a born leader. But will need the exacting demands of a great service to do justice to himself. His best is outstanding – his second best is not good enough.' Despite Hahn's reservations, he appointed Philip Gordonstoun's first 'Guardian', the title that was given to the Head Boy.

There could be no doubt about which direction Philip's career would take after Gordonstoun. Lord Mountbatten's father had been First Lord of the Admiralty and, in due course, Lord Louis would himself be appointed to this post. So, Philip went to Dartmouth Naval College where, in his first term, he won the King's Dirk as best cadet – where, too, he had that fateful meeting with the shy young Princess Elizabeth.

Marion Crawford later recalled how Elizabeth blushed deeply at the very sight of this 'fair-haired boy, rather like a Viking, with a sharp face and piercing blue eyes'. For Elizabeth it was love at first sight.

♛ *Princess Elizabeth happily riding a
Shetland pony on holiday in 1936*

♛ *The young Girl Guides. Margaret and
Elizabeth* right *in 1940 at Windsor Castle*

♛ *The teenage Elizabeth loved acting —
here she appears in Cinderella, at Windsor*

♛ *Sweet 16. Elizabeth wears the
uniform of a Colonel of the Grenadier Guards*

♛ *Aged 13, Elizabeth wins a
children's challenge shield for
the backstroke race*

♛ *Devoted sisters,
Elizabeth and Margaret at
the Royal Lodge, Windsor,
early in 1942*

Philip

👑 *The happy cricketer. Philip second from right at Gordonstoun in 1938*

Topham Picture Library

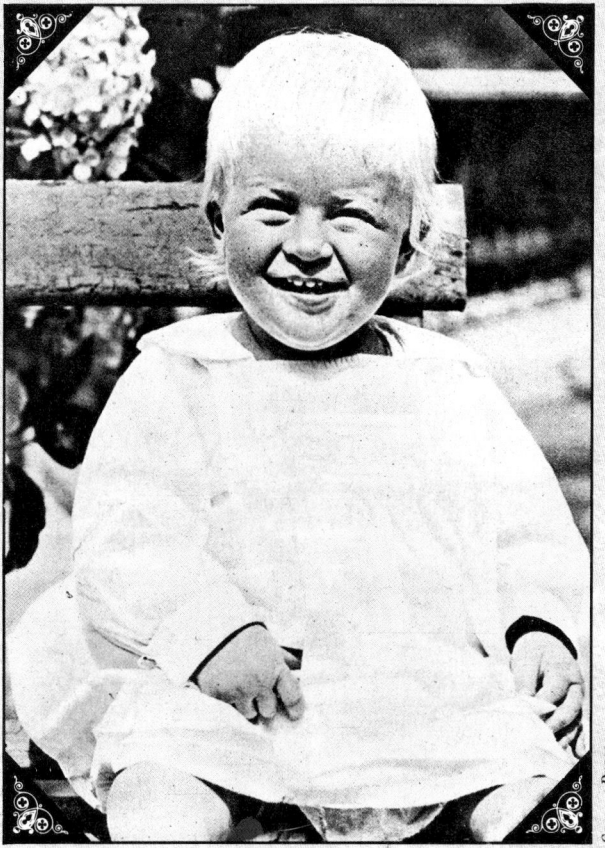

👑 *The young baby Philip, aged one, on holiday in Britain with his parents*

Camera Press

Popperfoto

👑 *Aged 14, the Prince takes to the boards in his school production of* Macbeth

Popperfoto

👑 *Relaxing on the water. Philip fools around in the school boat*

👑 *Archery practice for young Philip, aged eight second from left, at the St Cloud school in France*

Popperfoto

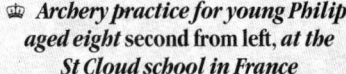

BUCKINGHAM PALACE

A national symbol, Buckingham Palace is the centre for ceremonial and State occasions. Thousands flock there at times of national rejoicing, or simply to see the Changing of the Guard, but few members of the public see inside the Palace. Dating from the time of George IV, when the original Buckingham House was enlarged by John Nash, further additions were made to house Queen Victoria's growing family. The familiar Portland stone façade was commissioned by King Edward VII

The Photographers Library

By gracious permission of HM the Queen

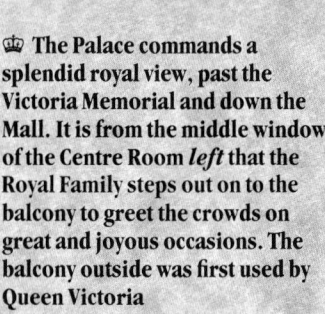

♛ The Palace commands a splendid royal view, past the Victoria Memorial and down the Mall. It is from the middle window of the Centre Room *left* that the Royal Family steps out on to the balcony to greet the crowds on great and joyous occasions. The balcony outside was first used by Queen Victoria

♛ The State Dining Room *right* dates from Victoria's reign – her cipher can still be seen in the medallion decorations. Above the chimney piece hangs a portrait of George IV by Sir Thomas Lawrence. This is flanked by paintings of other members of the Hanoverian Royal Family

♛ It is difficult to imagine that the pastoral scene *above* exists in the heart of London. This is the West front of the Palace, as it was designed by John Nash, which faces the landscaped garden

♛ Royal christenings take place in the beautiful Music Room *right* which retains its elegant John Nash style. It is decorated in ivory and gold, with 18 deep blue columns, a high domed ceiling and magnificent crystal chandeliers

♛ An original John Nash design, the Blue Drawing Room *above*, with its marble columns and ornamental ceiling, is considered to be the loveliest room in the Palace

♛ Overlooking the gardens and the lake, the 48-foot-long White Drawing Room *left* is where members of the Royal Family gather before State functions

♛ Majestically proportioned, the crimson and gold Throne Room *right*, dating from 1833, has a frieze depicting the Wars of the Roses

By gracious permission of HM the Queen

♔ 155 feet long and well lit by a domed glass ceiling, the Picture Gallery *above* houses the Queen's art collection, including works by Rembrandt, Van Dyck and Poussin

♔ In 1986, the Queen was seen by millions broadcasting from the Palace. One of the settings she chose was the Royal Mews, where all the ceremonial coaches and horses are housed *right*

BBC Enterprises

Hulton-Deutsch Collection

DIVIDED BY WAR

Popperfoto

PRINCESS ELIZABETH NEVER DOUBTED THAT PHILIP OF GREECE WAS TO BE THE LOVE OF HER LIFE. WHILE HE DISTINGUISHED HIMSELF DURING THE WAR, SHE WAITED PATIENTLY FOR THAT LOVE TO BE RETURNED

WAR-TORN EUROPE provided the harsh backdrop to the growing attachment between Elizabeth and Philip. When Britain declared war on Hitler's Germany on 3 September 1939, it was generally assumed that as the Royal Family made prime targets in the event of invasion, the young Princesses would be taken somewhere distant and safe – Canada, say – for the duration of hostilities. But the King and Queen, with their strong sense of duty, had no such intentions – the British first family would stay, come what may. As the Queen said: 'The children won't leave without me; I won't leave without the King; and the King will never leave.'

Firing ranges were improvised in the courtyards of Buckingham Palace and the Queen demonstrated her resolve by becoming an excellent pistol shot. 'I shall not go down like the others,' she remarked, referring to the assorted foreign Royals who regularly turned up on their doorstep asking for shelter and protection. And when the Palace was bombed in 1940 she was delighted – she was seen to be suffering the effects of war every bit as much as the humblest of her subjects.

The Princesses Elizabeth and Margaret were in Scotland when war was declared. Their governess was recalled from her annual holiday and sent to look after them, with instructions that life should proceed as normally as possible. For Elizabeth, this meant having to continue by post the study of British history she had begun

Hulton-Deutsch Collection

👑 *'I ought to do as other girls of my age do,' said Second Subaltern Elizabeth Windsor of her wartime training as army driver and car mechanic. She spent most of her stint in the ATS wearing overalls and covered in grease*

under the tutelage of Sir Henry Marten, Vice-Provost of Eton.

The Queen and her daughters missed each other so much that they made the brave – some said, foolhardy – decision to celebrate New Year together at Sandringham, despite the vulnerability of the East Anglian coast to invasion.

The problem remained of where the Princesses would stay during wartime. Windsor Castle – which had remained impregnable 'throughout its 900-year history – was selected, and it was there that Elizabeth and Margaret spent their teens. Officially, though, they were just 'somewhere in the country', and photographs were published showing the Royal Family looking happy in the middle of anonymous fields.

Midshipman Philip of Greece, RN, became a regular visitor to Windsor during his shore leaves. Perhaps a little ungallantly, he was to deny that he felt particularly strongly towards Elizabeth at this time. But they did begin to write to one another with increasing regularity, while she packed his photograph in her air-raid bag.

As a potential suitor to the heir to the Crown, Philip was peculiarly well placed. Queen Mary found him refreshing and accorded him the honour of being high on her 'knitting list', sending him scarves and socks. His Aunt Marina was Duchess of Kent, married to the King's youngest brother George, and he was frequently invited to their Buckinghamshire home, Coppins.

When the Duke of Kent was killed on

active service in 1941 Philip was among those who were particularly grief-stricken. But it was his Uncle 'Dickie', Lord Mountbatten, who remained his most trusted mentor and who profoundly approved of the match between Philip and Elizabeth. Rumours were now beginning to fly. As early as 1941, society diarist 'Chips' Channon wrote mischievously in one of his columns: 'Went to an enjoyable Greek cocktail party. Philip of Greece was there ... He is to be our Prince Consort, and that is why he is serving in our Navy.'

A special relationship

The King did not share Mountbatten's enthusiasm for the budding romance. As Elizabeth developed into a woman, he became fiercely protective of her – even a little jealous of the young men who competed for her attention. Although he had to admit that Elizabeth was in love with young Philip, and that a special relationship was growing between them, it still seemed inconceivable to the King that his elder daughter should fall in love with virtually the first man she had met, and he remained opposed to the match.

Elizabeth, meanwhile, had won one small battle against her father by insisting, in her polite, determined way, that she should be allowed to set an example by 'doing her bit' for the war effort. Accordingly, in 1944 she joined

THE BRAVE MIDSHIPMAN

Philip graduated from Dartmouth Naval College in 1940 and went straight into active service as a midshipman. He served on the battleship HMS *Valiant* at the landing of British troops on Crete, and for his action during the Battle of Matapan *below* he was mentioned in dispatches. He was made a First Lieutenant in 1944. At the end of the war, Philip looked forward to a long and successful career as a naval officer. It was a great disappointment to him when he had to cut short that career to fulfil royal duties

Popperfoto

Robert Hunt Library

♛ *Girl guiding and making a first radio broadcast relieved the austerity of wartime. The Royal Family also snatched happy interludes at Sandringham below*

Hulton-Deutsch Collection

the Auxiliary Territorial Service (ATS) as 'No. 230873 Second Subaltern Elizabeth Alexandra Mary Windsor. Age: 18. Hair: brown. Height: 5ft. 3ins.' She was a car mechanic.

She threw herself into stripping engines and driving lorries and became minutely absorbed in the workings of internal combustion engines. 'We had sparking plugs last night all through dinner,' the Queen said!

Elizabeth's army training was never to be put into practice, though, for the war officially ended at one minute past midnight on 8 May 1945, bringing to an end six years of suffering and uncertainty. The nation celebrated in extravagant fashion, and not even the thundery weather could dampen people's enthusiasm. Church bells rang out across London and tug boats on the River Thames sounded their horns in the Morse code letter V for Victory. Huge crowds thronged the West End and gathered outside the forecourt at Buckingham Palace to catch a glimpse of the Royal Family, and the Prime Minister, Winston Churchill. 'God bless you all,' Churchill told them. 'This is *your* victory.'

> ## 'It had been mentioned, presumably, that "He is eligible . . ." I must have been on the list, so to speak'
>
> PRINCE PHILIP

The King and Queen and the two Princesses stepped out repeatedly under arc lights to acknowledge the acclaim of the crowd. Then, with the King's permission, Elizabeth and Margaret, escorted by male relatives and army officers, sneaked quietly out of the Palace to join in the celebrations. For the first and the last time, they stood on the other side of the Palace gates, looking up and cheering with ordinary people.

A memorable night

Then, when their little party was swept along with the singing, dancing, shouting crowd, Elizabeth committed her one and only act of hooliganism – she knocked off a policeman's helmet. One of their 'gang', Mme de Ballaigue, recalled: 'On the whole we were not recognized. However, a Dutch serviceman, who attached himself to the end of our file of arm-in-arm people . . . realized who the Princesses were. He withdrew discreetly and just said, "It was a great honour. I shall never forget this evening."' Elizabeth called it 'one of the most memorable nights of my life'.

With the war over, the King could no longer avoid the question of his elder daughter's attachment to Philip. Elizabeth's photograph now went everywhere with the young naval officer,

and his was openly on show on her desk. When indiscretion was hinted at, she merely exchanged it for one of him wearing a beard.

Besides the King's opposition, Philip's nationality was a stumbling block to possible marriage. Was it tactful, at a time when Greece was torn by civil war between royalists and republicans, for a Greek prince to take the hand of the heir to the British Crown in marriage? And there was the problem of Philip's four sisters who were married to Germans and still living in Germany.

The King, who persisted in hoping that Elizabeth's ardour would cool, organized flocks of young men, mainly Guards officers, to escort his daughters to the new peacetime whirl of parties and balls. Queen Mary referred to them as the 'Body Guard' and for a while they successfully drew the fire of the media.

Events, however, soon moved out of the King's hands. During the Balmoral break of 1946 Prince Philip proposed to Elizabeth and, deeply in love, she accepted. The King was now forced to admit that Philip had his good points, and, as he enumerated in a letter to King George of Greece: 'He is intelligent, has a good sense of humour and thinks about things in the right way.'

The King began to initiate Philip into British royal customs. Invited to Balmoral for a grouse shoot, Philip turned up with a single small suitcase containing a second-hand dinner jacket, courtesy of Lord Mountbatten, one pair of flannels – and nothing suitable for tramping over the heather. The King, who approved of frugality, was happy to lend him a pair of plus-fours which Princess Margaret thought 'frightfully inelegant'. The King and his daughter's suitor found they had much in common, and gradually, over the months, the two became close.

Nevertheless, the war had robbed the Royal Family of six years of family life and the King felt deeply possessive towards his elder daughter. He insisted that the announcement of the engagement should be held back until 'Us Four', the Royal Family, had completed a long-proposed tour of South Africa. He thought it was possible that Elizabeth might think differently after the trip, although in his heart he knew that his elder daughter had never vacillated over anything – this love to her was everything, and not easily diverted.

WARTIME AT WINDSOR

Windsor Castle – bristling with barbed wire and spiked with anti-aircraft guns – was home to the two Princesses during the war. Lessons continued as normal, as did the King's instruction of Elizabeth in State affairs. Rationing was also observed – a five-inch line was painted on all the Royal baths – while the dungeons doubled as air-raid shelters. The high spots of this drab existence were pantomimes, when the Princesses made the most of the dressing-up boxes. One performance in 1943 saw Elizabeth in a particularly vivacious mood – Philip of Greece just happened to be in the front row of the audience! But life at Windsor was generally rather trying during the war, and the castle became a virtual prison to the young Princesses, despite the splendour of the surroundings. 'Poor darlings, they have never had any fun yet,' said the King on VE day

NEWLY BETROTHED

The Royal Family set sail on HMS *Vanguard* on 1 February 1947 on what was to be a triumphant, if gruelling, tour. Not surprisingly, Elizabeth often looked distracted – it was a long time to be away from the man she loved and intended to marry. She was in Cape Town when she celebrated her 21st birthday on 21 April 1947. She broadcast a heartfelt speech to the Empire that day: 'I declare before you that my whole life, whether it be long or short, shall be devoted to your service . . . But I shall not have the strength to carry out this resolution unless you join in it with me, as I now invite you to do; I know that your support will be unfailingly given. God bless all of you who are willing to share it.'

The King's blessing

Philip meanwhile had become a naturalized British citizen (after some adroit string-pulling by Lord Mountbatten, who stressed that his protégé 'has been brought up as an Englishman who rides well, shoots well and plays all games such as football with more than usual ability'). When he renounced his Greek title and took the surname of his British uncle, the last stumbling block to his marriage to Elizabeth had been removed.

Back home, on 8 July 1947, Elizabeth confided to a friend: 'Something is going to happen at last. He is coming tonight.' Two days later the Palace issued a statement: 'It is with the greatest pleasure that the King and Queen announce the betrothal of their dearly beloved daughter, the Princess Elizabeth, to Lieutenant Philip Mountbatten, RN, son of the late Prince Andrew of Greece and Princess Andrew (Princess Alice of Battenberg), to which union The King has gladly given his consent.'

Popperfoto

Hulton-Deutsch Collection

☙ *A garden party at Buckingham Palace marked the announcement of the Royal engagement* left *and below. Intense press speculation had been confirmed. According to Philip, it was not until 1946, at Balmoral, that the couple had seriously discussed getting married, although Elizabeth's grandmother said they had been in love for 18 months before that. 'She won't give her heart lightly, but when she does it will be for always,' Queen Mary had remarked presciently. The couple were formally engaged on 10 July 1947* right

JOYFUL SECRET

The State visit to South Africa in 1947 was a tremendously happy occasion for the Royal Family. Elizabeth was particularly radiant – throughout the gruelling tour a smile was never far from her lips. Philip had already proposed, she had accepted, and soon the whole world would know of their impending marriage

Popperfoto

Popperfoto

Diamond fringe tiara, dating from 1830, holding a fine tulle veil

Two strings of pearls, both wedding gifts

Baron/Camera Press

♛ Norman Hartnell based the beautiful pearl and crystal embroidery adorning Elizabeth's dress on a painting by Botticelli in the National Gallery. The classic gown, with its fitted bodice, full skirt and 15-foot-long train, was made of ivory duchesse satin

Bouquet of white orchids and sprigs of myrtle

Garlands of York roses, syringa and jasmine with star flowers

THE 'BOTTICELLI' BRIDE

Princess Elizabeth spent her teenage years in wartime, when the fashion industry hardly existed. Girls dressed like their mothers and the cult of youth had not yet started. Times were still austere when she married, but her wedding dress brought back a touch of Renaissance magic to a glamour-starved public. As Queen, fashion has never been a high priority for Elizabeth. Her mother's designer, Norman Hartnell, made many of the clothes shown here – which date from the early years of her reign

Beret-style hat with dyed ostrich feather trim

lightly padded shoulders

Inset bands on cross over bodice, held by buttons

narrow skirt with three inset pleats at one side

Hemline 14 inches from the ground

Hulton-Deutsch Collection

👑 Two Hartnell designs for the Royal couple's 1954 visit to Australasia. *Left* An afternoon dress in silk shantung and *below* an evening dress in white lace, threaded with silver

Hulton-Deutsch Collection

👑 Elizabeth's going-away outfit is far more formal in style than any 21-year-old would wear today. The dress is in love-in-a-mist blue crêpe, worn with a beret-style hat trimmed with feather pompons

👑 The Queen's evening gowns, like this Hartnell style, are always designed to support the Garter riband at the shoulder

Hulton-Deutsch Collection

lumberjack style checked shirt

High, tight-fitting waistband

Deep roll collar and single button fastening on jacket

👑 A visit to Canada in 1951 gave Elizabeth and Philip the chance to join a lively square dance. Her circular skirt and casual shirt are just right for the occasion

Slim-fitting collarless shirt in matching tweed

Contrasting appliqué on circular skirt

👑 The Queen has always felt happiest in tweeds. She wore this elegant three-piece for the Olympic Horse Trials at Windsor in 1955

High-heeled, peep-toed court shoes

♛ Off-the-face hat styles of the 1950s – the low-crowned shapes are good for getting out of cars

♛ A simple reversible tweed coat, perfect for the Braemar Games, worn with a feathered beret which gives a playful air. Philip adds his own fashion touch with a kilt

Reginald Davies

Halter-style shoulder strap

♛ One of Hartnell's most successful designs – a brilliantly simple evening dress in black and white satin for the Royal Command film performance in 1951

Contrasting white satin panel, shaped to emphasise the waist

Above the elbow gloves

THE ILLUSTRATED LONDON NEWS
ROYAL WEDDING NUMBER

John Frost

MARRIED IN STATE

ON A GREY, RAINSWEPT DAY IN NOVEMBER 1947, WAR-WEARY BRITAIN WAS REINVIGORATED BY THE ROYAL WEDDING. PEOPLE CROWDED THE STREETS TO JOIN IN ELIZABETH AND PHILIP'S NEW-FOUND HAPPINESS

ELIZABETH AND PHILIP HAD WAITED SO long to make public their love that it seemed only fair to be granted an early wedding. The date was fixed for 20 November 1947, four and a half months away from the engagement announcement.

The Royal Family had to exercise considerable diplomacy over every aspect of the great day. Royal wedding it may have been, but it was also an austerity celebration. The Palace had to tread a very thin line between unacceptable ostentation and equally unacceptable drabness. But Winston Churchill put their minds at rest, saying the festivities would be 'a flash of colour on the hard road we have to travel'.

While Elizabeth organized her new staff, appointing ladies-in-waiting, and Jock Colville as her private secretary, her governess, Marion Crawford, was herself married. The Princesses were sad to see her leave the Royal household, but Marion Crawford did not endear herself to the Royal Family when, three years later, she went into print with revelations of her time as governess to Elizabeth and Margaret. She had broken Royal protocol and her name was never mentioned again within Royal circles.

Before the ceremony

There were upheavals of greater note in the outside world, notably the loss of India from the British Empire. It was nursed towards Independence by its last Viceroy, Earl Mountbatten of Burma – Philip's 'Uncle Dickie'. He was appointed early in 1947. It was a traumatic birth for the new State and the pangs were felt very strongly at the Palace.

In September, Philip was received into the Anglican Church, of which his wife would one day be head. And in November, Elizabeth and Philip were created Knights of the Garter by her proud father.

Prince Philip's stag night at London's Dorchester Hotel was a high-spirited and distinctly naval affair. Philip's best man was David, Marquess of Milford Haven, his cousin and friend from childhood – and another Mountbatten. The Earl himself presided over his protégé's festivities.

But the occasion was marred for Philip by the intrusion of the press. Finally, Uncle Dickie did a deal with the photographers – they agreed to hand over their cameras and allow pictures to be taken of themselves. It may have seemed an odd arrangement, but few men ever quibbled with Earl Mountbatten. When the cameras were handed over, guests went through the motions of taking photographs of the Fleet Street 'rat pack', but then the flash

♔ Street sellers were doing a good trade in selling streamers and balloons on 19 November 1947, the night before Elizabeth and Philip's wedding. People were willing to stay up all night to make sure of a good viewing position on the wedding route

Topham Picture Library

bulbs were ripped out and smashed, effectively ending the night's entertainment for the photographers. It was ruthless, but it worked.

A mountain of gifts

Thousands of wedding presents had been pouring in since the couple's engagement and a selection were on view at St James's Palace. Among the china and table lamps was a humble piece of cloth: it had been woven from thread spun by Mahatma Gandhi specially for Princess Elizabeth, at the suggestion of Earl Mountbatten. But when Queen Mary and other members of the Royal Family came to preview the presents it proved controversial. The old Queen thought it was a loincloth, and Prince Philip's attempts to explain the gift by describing Gandhi as 'a great man' proved in vain – Queen Mary sailed past without a word. At the next Royal inspection, Princess Margaret managed to dash ahead of the Queen and hide Gandhi's humble gift behind other presents.

Sensible gifts came too, such as an electric cleaning machine from Hoover Ltd and an early type of washing machine given by the people of Leamington Spa. But a particular favourite of Elizabeth's was the very practical picnic basket given to her by her sister.

Four of the most valuable presents were not on show. The Kenyan people had given the couple Sagana Hunting Lodge – which was, later, to play such a significant and poignant role in their lives, while the Aga Khan went straight to the Princess's heart by giving her a racehorse called Astrakhan. But most magnificent of all were her parents' gifts of a diamond and ruby necklace (which she was to wear many times), and a ribbon-bow brooch made of diamonds given to her by Queen Mary.

Only a relatively small area of bomb-scarred London was decorated for the occasion, but the route between Buckingham Palace and Westminster Abbey was bedecked with yellow and white bunting bearing burgundy-coloured motifs of entwined 'E's and 'P's, and royal blue banners hung close to the Palace. It was not to be a public holiday, declared the Prime Minister, Clement Attlee. But there was to be glamour – the Household Cavalry were permitted to wear full ceremonial dress for the first time in six years.

Wedding day dawns

On the morning of 20 November, the rain held off – a mercy to the thousands who had slept in the streets hoping to secure a good view of the procession – but the sky was overcast.

Before the wedding, the King summoned Philip and gave him the titles of Duke of Edinburgh, Earl of Merioneth and Baron Greenwich. (Philip had ceased to be a Prince of

In austere post-war Britain, no bank holiday was declared for the Royal wedding. But to the crowds who lined the streets, it seemed just like one. Boy Scouts helped to sell wedding programmes to celebrate the first Royal wedding since that of the bride's own parents

WEDDING DAY

After a few last-minute panics to mend Elizabeth's tiara and find her wedding bouquet, she arrived calmly at Westminster Abbey with her father *below, far left*. As she entered the Abbey, her bridesmaids, including her sister Margaret, helped to prepare her long veil and train *left* . She walked up the aisle with her father to join Philip for the marriage ceremony *below*, which was conducted by the Archbishop of Canterbury in the sacrarium in front of their families. Many other foreign guests and dignitaries watched the service from the main part of the Abbey

Hulton-Deutsch Collection

Greece on his naturalization and was not to be created a British prince until 1957.)

Elizabeth was woken as usual with a cup of Earl Grey tea, and then began the solemn business of dressing for her wedding. The self-effacing Princess was silent during the fitting of her dress but as she saw herself in all her glory she burst out, 'It really is lovely!'

Norman Hartnell had cancelled an important trip to the United States to give himself time to design the perfect wedding dress. He found his inspiration in the National Gallery, in a Botticelli painting. The dress, created in a workroom with whitewashed windows to keep out prying eyes, was a simple, classic outline in ivory duchesse satin, garlanded with pearls and crystal. The skirt was decorated with white York roses and wheatears made from lavishly applied seed pearls.

Her silk train, which was 15 feet long, had been made at an English silkworm farm. It was held at the Princess's shoulders to avoid putting too much strain on the headband or tiara, and her bridal veil was kept in place by a diamond and pearl diadem, especially chosen from the Royal jewels.

There were some last-minute problems: no-one could find the bouquet until an enterprising footman found it keeping cool in a refrigerator. The pearl necklace was also missing – it was still on display at St James's Palace and was only retrieved by a fraught Jock Colville after he had battled his way through the security men on guard. Then the tiara snapped, requiring some swift improvised surgery. But nothing could disturb the bride's composure.

The Royal ceremony

Elizabeth left Buckingham Palace at 11.16 am and set off beside her father on her ceremonial ride to Westminster Abbey. They were escorted all the way by a Sovereign's Escort of the Household Cavalry in full dress. As the bride and her father entered the Abbey, the Kneller Hall trumpeters burst forth with *Praise My Soul, The King of Heaven*. Newsreel cameras, discreetly hidden behind a specially constructed plaster partition, recorded the event for posterity. As she walked up the aisle, the bride was attended by eight bridesmaids, including her sister Princess Margaret, Lady Pamela Mountbatten and Princess Alexandra. Her young pages were Prince William of Gloucester and Prince Michael of Kent. In his address, the Archbishop of Canterbury told the congregation that they were witnessing a ceremony which was 'exactly the same as it would be for any commoner who might be married this afternoon in some small country church in a remote village in the dales . . .'

As she left the Abbey, Princess Elizabeth

🎗 *As the newly married couple left the Abbey to the strains of Mendelssohn's* Wedding March, *they were greeted by a tumultuous roar from the waiting crowds who had all been listening to the broadcast wedding service*

made a very moving gesture when she stopped in the aisle and gave a deep curtsey to her father, who was visibly touched by the love transparent in her face as she did so. And as her mother had done at her own wedding, Princess Elizabeth laid her bouquet on the tomb of the Unknown Warrior as a humble gesture to those who had lost their lives in the war.

Among the guests present at the ceremony were the station master from Wolferton, near Sandringham; the Princesses' former riding teacher; and the 20 seamstresses who had

made the wedding dress. Those conspicuous by their absence included the Duke of Windsor (Uncle David) and his wife, Philip's 'German' sisters – and nightclub singer Hélène Cordet, a childhood friend of Philip's and one of the few women of whom Princess Elizabeth was known to be jealous. She had allegedly crossed off Hélène Cordet's name from the guest list.

As the couple came out of the Abbey, they were greeted by the cheering crowds. They travelled to Buckingham Palace in the Glass Coach, happily waving from the window to all the people that lined the route.

A simple celebration

A modest 150 guests attended the wedding breakfast in the gold and white supper room at Buckingham Palace. A sprig of white heather was placed beside each plate, while the room blazed with bowls of carnations sent by the British Carnation Society. Guests also found sprigs of myrtle by their plates, cuttings from the bush grown from Queen Victoria's bridal bouquet. The meal was simple and short. They ate sole followed by partridge, and then ice cream, to a medley of tunes played by pipers from Balmoral and the band of the Grenadier Guards.

The magnificent wedding cake was again made by McVitie and Price Ltd – they had also been given the honour of making the cake for Elizabeth's mother. The cake was 9 feet high, weighed 500 pounds and had four tiers. The tiers were decorated with the armorial bearings of the bride and groom and scenes from the life of the Royal couple. A vase of white camellias and roses topped the cake. The cake was cut by the couple with Philip's sword as part of the normal naval tradition.

The wedding celebrations over, the newlyweds stepped out on to the Buckingham Palace balcony to present themselves to the patient crowds and then retreated to submit to wedding photographs.

There could be no doubting the happiness of Elizabeth and Philip. The King was frankly worried, however. That day, he confided to a fellow guest: 'I wonder if Philip knows what he is taking on. One day Lilibet will be Queen and he will be Consort. That's much harder than being King, but I think he's the man for the job.'

Off on honeymoon

After being called out on to the balcony three times by the rapturous crowd, the newly created Duchess of Edinburgh changed into a simple blue crêpe coat and matching velour hat. It was a chilly evening as she and Philip climbed into their open carriage but thick travelling rugs covered their knees, and under them were hot water bottles – and Elizabeth's favourite corgi, Susan. Showered with rose petals by their relatives and friends, they drove through the still-festive streets to Waterloo Station. From there the honeymooners went by Royal Train to the seclusion of Broadlands, the Hampshire home of the Mountbattens which had been kindly lent to them.

A father's sentiments

That day the King handed Elizabeth a letter containing his heartfelt thoughts:

'I was so proud of you and thrilled at having you close to me on our long walk in Westminster Abbey, but when I handed your hand to the Archbishop I felt that I had lost something very precious. You were so calm and composed during the Service and said your words with such conviction, that I knew it was all right . . .' Then followed what seemed to be an explanation – an apology for his initial attitude towards the wedding. 'I am so glad you wrote and told Mummy that you think the long wait before your engagement and the long time before the wedding was for the best. I was rather afraid that you had thought I was being hard-hearted about it . . . Our family, Us Four, the "Royal Family" must remain together with additions, of course, at suitable moments!! I have watched you grow up all these years with pride under the skilful direction of Mummy, who as you know is the most marvellous person in the world in my eyes, and I can, I know, always count on you, and now Philip, to help us in our work . . . I can see that you are sublimely happy with Philip which is right. But don't forget us is the wish of your ever loving and devoted PAPA.'

No one has recorded Princess Elizabeth's reaction to this letter, but it has remained one of her treasured possessions.

The reporters intrude

There was no official reception for the couple as they arrived at Broadlands – at their request, but crowds had waited outside the house, to greet them.

The servants at Broadlands had discreetly departed that evening. The first night of Elizabeth and Philip's married life was spent in a massive four-poster bed made cosy behind draped curtains. Their room overlooked the River Test and commanded a sweeping view of the countryside.

But the Edinburghs' seclusion was illusory. When they went to church at Romsey Abbey, they were pestered by scores of reporters and cameramen. It was simply too much for them to take. Their Broadlands honeymoon abruptly ended and the lovers fled to Birkhall, on the Balmoral estate in Scotland, to be alone: at last they could learn about each other and ponder on what the future might hold for them.

Topham Picture Library

♔ *To cries of 'We want the bride', Elizabeth and Philip reappeared on the Palace balcony* above *with from left to right the King, Princess Margaret, Lady Cambridge, the Queen and Queen Mary. Later, their peaceful honeymoon at* Broadlands *was spoiled by the press when they attended church at Romsey Abbey. Desperate for some time to be alone together, they left Broadlands and retreated to the quiet seclusion of Balmoral*

Hulton-Deutsch Collection

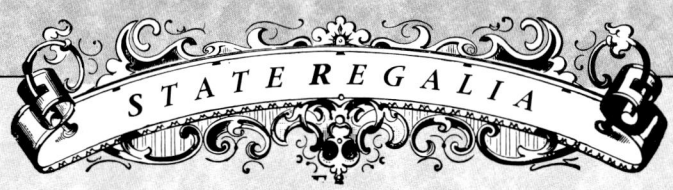

STATE REGALIA

THE ELIZABETHAN TRADITION

Royal ceremonial plays an important part in the traditions of the United Kingdom. For sheer spectacle, there is nothing to compare with the sight of the glittering Gold State Coach, travelling at a stately walking pace with its escort of red-coated postilions. More symbolism is represented by St Edward's Crown, the Jewelled Sword and the New Armills, which were a gift to the Queen from the people of the Commonwealth

Hulton-Deutsch Collection

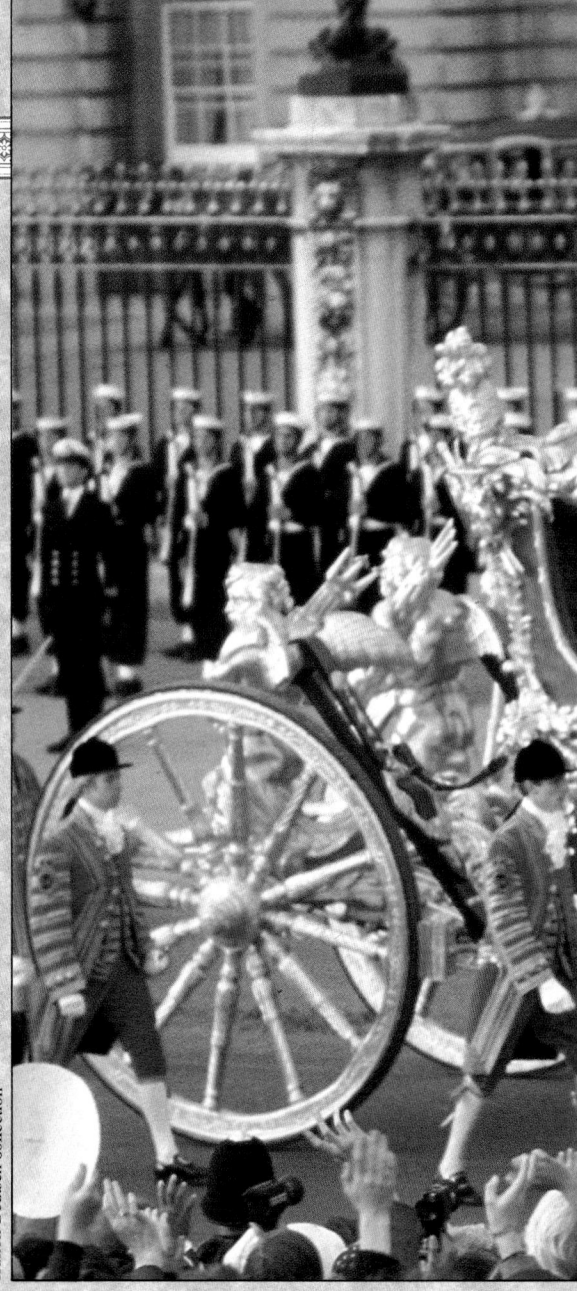

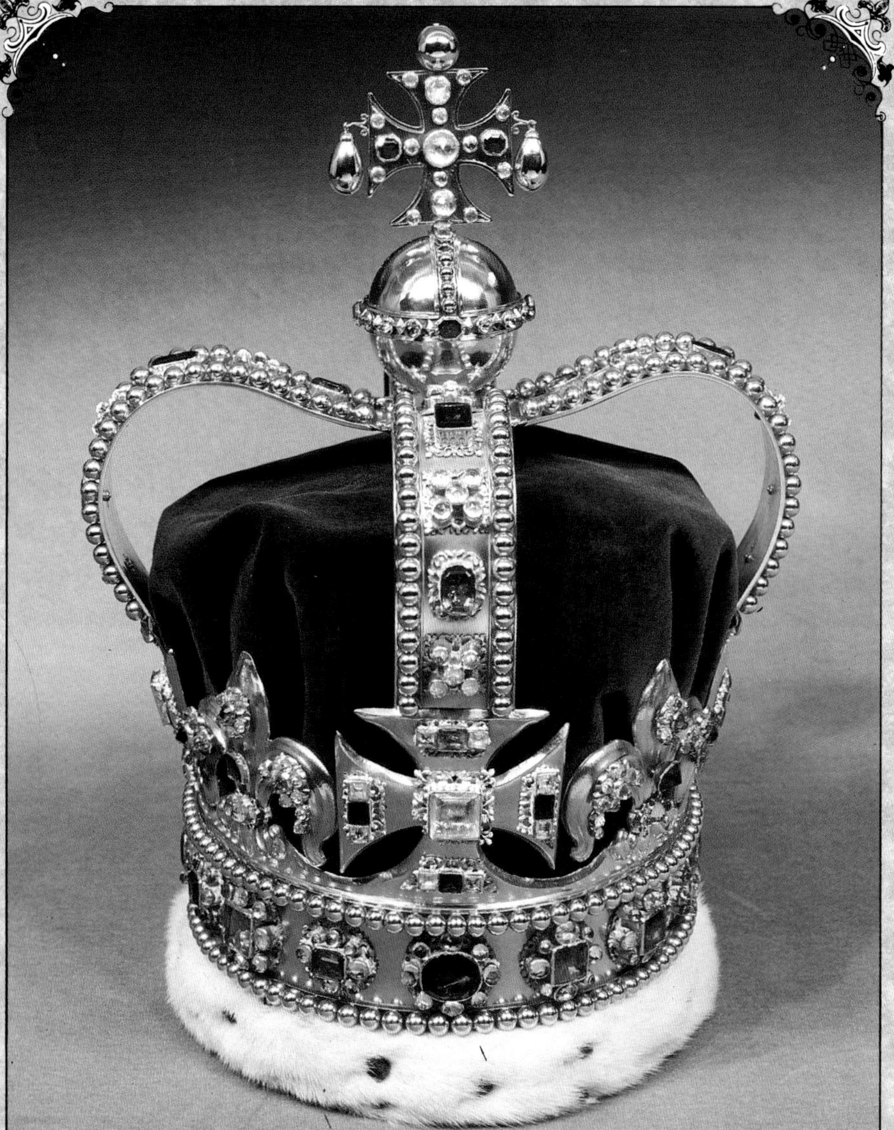

ST EDWARD'S CROWN

Dating from the Coronation of King Charles II and reset for King George V, this crown, which weighs five and a half pounds, is studded with over 400 precious and semi-precious stones. It was used at the climax of the ceremony for the actual crowning of the Queen

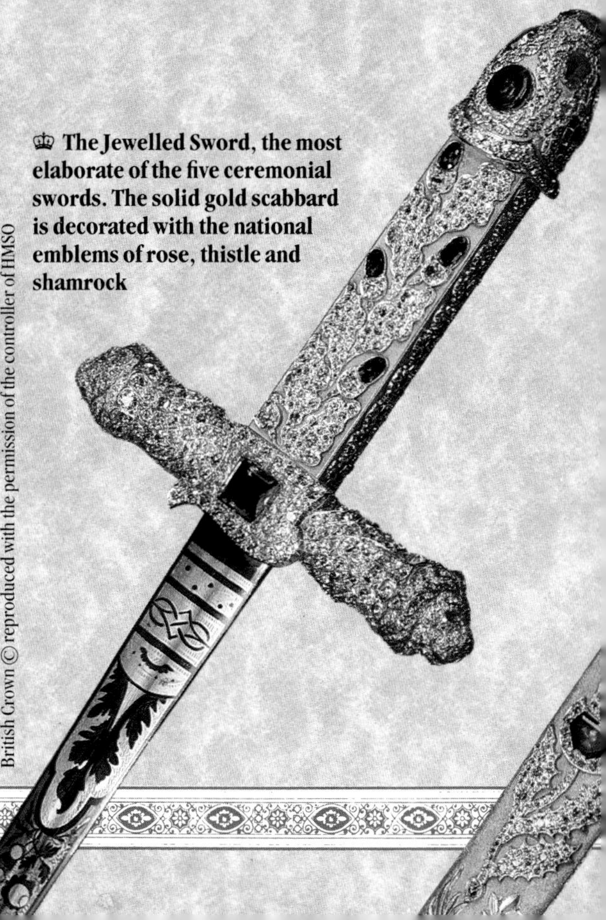

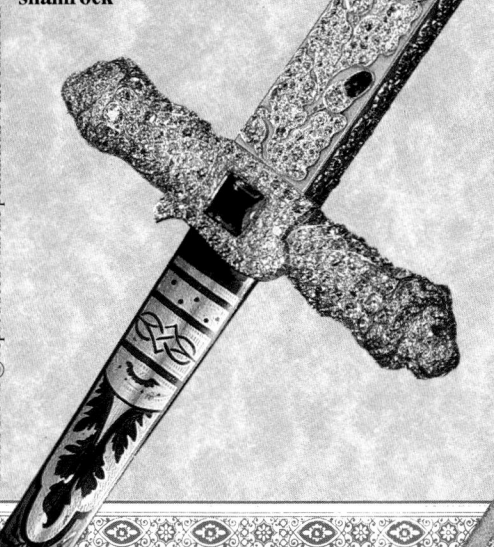

The Jewelled Sword, the most elaborate of the five ceremonial swords. The solid gold scabbard is decorated with the national emblems of rose, thistle and shamrock

British Crown © reproduced with the permission of the controller of HMSO

🖐 The Gold State Coach *above* has been used for every coronation since that of George IV in 1820, as well as for other occasions such as the State Opening of Parliament. It is 24 feet long and 12 feet high, richly carved with symbolic figures *right*. The painted panels *top right* are by Giovanni Battista Cipriani, a Florentine artist who came to London in 1755. The coach is drawn by eight bay horses

By gracious permission of HM the Queen

🖐 The New Armills, or 'bracelets of sincerity and wisdom', are shown *left*. Each bracelet, in pure gold, weighs four and a half ounces and is one and a half inches wide. The original Armills were carried in procession, but the Queen wore hers lined in velvet for comfort

Baron/Camera Press

A NEW ROYAL FAMILY

THE NEWLYWEDS ENJOYED FIVE CAREFREE YEARS TOGETHER DURING WHICH CHARLES AND ANNE WERE BORN. ON 6 FEBRUARY 1952, THE KING DIED TRAGICALLY EARLY AND WITHIN 16 MONTHS ELIZABETH WAS CROWNED QUEEN

PRINCESS ELIZABETH LOST NO TIME IN producing a son and heir. Within three months of her marriage, she was pregnant. Supremely happy though she was, however, her condition was to exacerbate the stresses of the Edinburghs' first tour abroad – to Paris in 1948. Her Private Secretary, Jock Colville, recalled, 'Far too many people were asked to every single function.' Camera lenses were everywhere – even, on one occasion, hidden in the middle of a table in an otherwise empty room. Philip was furious, but his wife kept smiling.

On Sunday, 14 November 1948, Sir William Gilliatt, the top gynaecologist, and Sister Helen Rowe, a midwife, were on hand for the imminent birth, while beyond the Palace railings a large crowd waited anxiously for news. As evening fell, Elizabeth went into labour and her husband worked off his tension in an energetic game of squash with his equerry and long-standing friend, Michael Parker.

A Prince is born

At 9.14 pm, the Princess gave birth to a boy. When she came round from the anaesthetic, Philip presented her with an enormous bouquet of carnations and roses, while cheering could be heard from the Mall. The new mother studied her first-born carefully, exclaiming at his 'fine long fingers, quite unlike mine and certainly unlike his father's'.

The next day, official celebrations for the future king began with loyal toasts, deafening gun salutes and fountains that foamed with blue water for the whole week. The focus of this festivity lay quietly in his cot, marvelled over by his mother, who wrote to a friend: 'It's wonderful to think, isn't it, that his arrival could give a bit of happiness to so many people, besides ourselves, at this time?'

The Royal baby was christened in the Music Room at Buckingham Palace. Charles Philip

Cecil Beaton/Camera Press

Topham Picture Library

The Princ In Malt

ILLUSTRATED

👑 *For a few precious months on Malta, Elizabeth led a relatively normal life, picnicking, sunbathing and chatting with other naval wives. The occasional photocalls were a reminder, if any were needed, that she was no ordinary young woman*

Cecil Beaton/Camera Press

👑 *The newborn Charles left looked 'like a plum pudding,' joked Philip, while his proud mother doted on her first son. Two years later Anne was born above and Charles had a sister – 'the sweetest girl,' according to her gallant father*

Arthur George sailed serenely through the ceremony, wearing the traditional robe originally worn by Queen Victoria's children.

Elizabeth and Philip kept a suite at Buckingham Palace and for a time rented Windlesham Moor in Berkshire. The house they had set their hearts on, Sunninghill Park near Windsor, had burnt down before they could move in. By now, Parliament had voted Philip £10,000 a year, while his wife received £50,000. In addition, as a lieutenant, Philip had his salary from the Royal Navy.

A naval career

In 1949, Philip was seconded to the First Cruiser Squadron in the Mediterranean as First Lieutenant of HMS *Chequers,* the leading ship of Earl Mountbatten's fleet. He was only one step away from his burning ambition, the command of his own ship. But this was soon to be achieved and by 1950 he was in full command of his own ship, HMS *Magpie*. A naval posting at Malta followed, which was to be the most 'ordinary' life Elizabeth and Philip were to know together. They lived, by courtesy of Earl Mountbatten, in the Villa Guardamangia surrounded by exotic and fragrant shrubs. Then, while Charles remained at home with his grandparents – 'he is too sweet stumping around the room,' the King declared – Elizabeth and Philip toured the Mediterranean.

This was a splendid opportunity for Philip to introduce his wife to the beautiful land of his birth. In Athens, they saw the sights – including the floodlit Parthenon, paid a visit to Philip's cousins, the King and Queen of Greece, and spent a riotous evening in the British Ambassador's beach house. The Edinburghs also visited Rome, where the first serious criticisms of Elizabeth's lack of chic were made, though this, characteristically, hardly troubled her. Throughout the tour, she was in sparkling mood, happy in her marriage and – to her great delight – pregnant once again.

Princess Anne Elizabeth Alice Louise was born at Clarence House on 15 August 1950, a few months after Elizabeth and Philip returned to England.

Anne was a controversial choice for a first name; George V had loathed it but Elizabeth and Philip thought it pretty. 'Elizabeth' honoured the baby's mother and her mother; 'Alice' paid tribute to Philip's mother, and 'Louise' was after the Queen of Sweden, a close friend of Elizabeth and Philip. The Edinburghs' happiness was complete. Although official duties occupied much of their attention, the important part of every day was the time spent in the nursery. Elizabeth insisted on bathing the children and putting them to bed herself, where she would read to them as the Queen had read to her.

At the time of Prince Charles's birth, King George VI had finally submitted to an examination of his increasingly painful legs; arteriosclerosis was diagnosed and for a time it even seemed that his right leg might have to be

Popperfoto

Hulton-Deutsch Collection

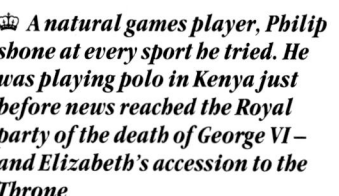
♔ *A natural games player, Philip shone at every sport he tried. He was playing polo in Kenya just before news reached the Royal party of the death of George VI – and Elizabeth's accession to the Throne*

amputated. Although the leg was saved, the King remained poorly and, during 1951, his health deteriorated rapidly. Cancer was diagnosed, and on 23 September he was operated on: his left lung was removed to try to prevent the spread of the disease.

As a precaution against the King's death, when the Edinburghs set out on their tour of the United States and Canada in early October 1951, Elizabeth carried in her luggage her mourning attire – and a sealed envelope containing her Accession papers. The visit was a qualified success. An estimated 500,000 people lined the streets of Quebec, but Philip upset some people by referring to Canada as a 'good investment', while Elizabeth was criticized in the Press for looking glum and for leaving her children behind. The USA, however, loved them. In a letter to the King, President Truman enthused, 'They went to the hearts of all the citizens of the United States . . . As one father to another we can be very proud of our daughters, you have the better of me – because you have two.'

The shadow of ill-health still hung over the King. Although, on 29 January 1952, his doctors had declared themselves pleased at his

Hulton-Deutsch Collection

'satisfactory progress', a quick deterioration followed. Some time in the early hours of 6 February 1952, King George VI died.

A new Queen

Elizabeth II became Queen as she spent the night in a treetop observation hide, known as 'Treetops', near the Sagana Hunting Lodge in Kenya. The hide overlooked a watering hole illuminated by floodlights, and she watched and photographed in fascination as a succession of exotic animals came to the hole to drink.

When the Edinburghs' staff heard the news of the King's death, Philip's equerry, Michael Parker, took him to one side and told him quietly. 'He looked,' Parker said later, 'as if you'd dropped half the world on him. I never felt so sorry for anyone in my life.'

Philip broke the news to the new Queen as they walked together by the watering hole. Then they retired out of sight. When Elizabeth reappeared, the immaculate royal training was in evidence. She immediately composed and sent the necessary telegrams and distributed farewell presents among their African servants. When asked what name she would choose as Queen, she replied simply, 'My own name – what else?'

On her return to London, Elizabeth was met at Heathrow Airport by the Duke of Gloucester, Clement Attlee, Anthony Eden and Winston Churchill. 'This is a tragic homecoming,' she said briefly.

👑 *Elizabeth and Philip enjoyed barely five years of close-knit family life before she was to take on the onerous responsibilities of the monarch. Behind the smiles of their North American tour of 1951* above, *there was already grave concern for George VI's failing health. He died on 6 February 1952 while the Royal couple were in Kenya. Elizabeth returned to England as Queen* below

Hulton-Deutsch Collection

Popperfoto

Hulton-Deutsch Collection

Rex Features

CORONATION FEVER

Coronation Day, 2 June 1953, was marked by an eruption of patriotic fervour. Although the skies were grey, the crowds lined the streets from early in the morning *above*. Everyone was determined to celebrate the dawn of a new era – and they did, at parties throughout the country. Neighbourhoods crowned their own 'queens' and sat down to sumptuous coronation suppers, while souvenir-hunters bought anything from coronation storybooks to mugs *below*. An estimated 20 million people watched Elizabeth on their screens as she accepted the sceptre and crown from the Archbishop of Canterbury *top centre* and *right*, before walking down the aisle to emerge as Queen *top right*. For the Queen herself, the ceremony, and the presence of the television cameras, were a test of her composure that she passed with flying colours

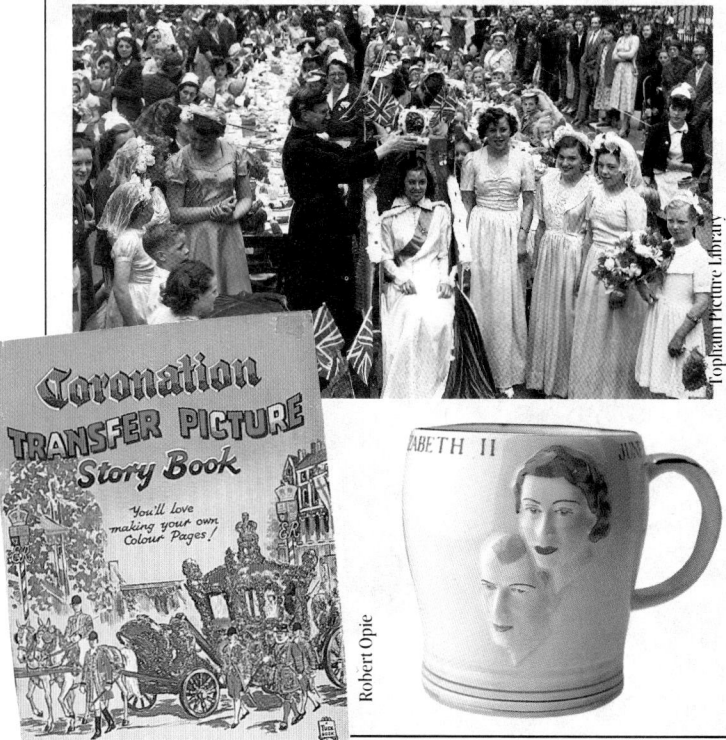

Topham Picture Library

Robert Opie

Hulton–Deutsch Collection

Cecil Beaton/Camera Press

OUR SOVEREIGN QUEEN

Only once in that first week did Queen Elizabeth betray her grief. Following the distress of attending her father's lying-in-state with her mother, grandmother and sister, came the funeral itself. It was only after making her Accession speech, in which she said, 'My heart is too full for me to say more to you today than that I shall always work as my father did,' that she wept on her husband's shoulder in the back of their car.

Queen Mary, who had lived through the death of three sons and the abdication of her eldest, helped sort out matters of ritual and tradition enshrined in the Coronation ceremony. Frail and poorly, however, she was not to see the new Queen crowned. She died on 24 March 1953 and was buried next to her husband, George V, in St George's Chapel, Windsor.

The ceremony

Elizabeth had learned much of the intricate and ancient symbolism of the Coronation as a 10-year-old when her parents took on the awesome responsibility of the Crown. That responsibility was now hers and it was to be hers alone, for, due to a quirk in the British Constitution, wives of the monarch automatically became Queen Consorts, but husbands do not become Kings.

Due to the immense problems involved in staging such an enormous spectacle, there were a full 16 months between the Accession and the Coronation of Elizabeth II, during which Elizabeth carefully studied the rites involved with the help of the Archbishop of Canterbury.

The Coronation had to be right in every detail, for it was to be televised live (despite reservations from Winston Churchill, among others, who thought the strain on the new Queen would be too great). Elizabeth also insisted on wearing the enormously heavy St Edward's Crown, rather than the lighter Imperial State Crown which had been worn by Queen Victoria at her Coronation. To get used to it, she wore a crown 'around the house' for a few days before the ceremony.

On 2 June 1953, thousands of people stood several deep along the route from Buckingham Palace to Westminster Abbey. Decorative arches and crowns hung above central London and

> ## '*My heart is too full for me to say more than that I shall always work as my father did*'
> QUEEN ELIZABETH II

bunting was out the length and breadth of the country. Even rain could not dampen people's spirits. Coronation fever had hit Britain.

The Coronation ceremony consists of five parts: the Recognition, the Oath, the Anointing, the Investiture and the Homage. It serves to present the Monarch to the people, to anoint her before God, and to allow her subjects to swear their allegiance.

At 11.15 am, Elizabeth entered the Abbey from the specially constructed awning over the West Door. The Archbishop of Canterbury, Geoffrey Fisher, led her to the four corners of the Abbey, presenting her with the words, 'Queen Elizabeth, your undoubted Queen'. The response was a heartfelt 'God save Queen Elizabeth!' Then, the Queen took the Oath, promising to govern according to the established laws and the precedents of the Church.

After this, her ladies ritually removed all the outward signs of her worldly status, covering the glittering robe with a plain white overgarment to signify humility before her people. (Elizabeth forgot to remove her earrings – the only mistake she made in the four-hour ceremony.)

Then followed the Anointing. The Archbishop intoned, 'Be thy hands anointed with holy oil, be thy breast anointed with holy oil, be thy head anointed with holy oil,' as he symbolically touched the monarch lightly with the anointing spoon.

Elizabeth then stood to be dressed in the symbols of her office – a white tunic under a cloth-of-gold outer garment. Seated in King Edward's Chair, she was given the Armills, bracelets specially made for this coronation, which symbolized sincerity and wisdom; the Golden Spurs, symbolizing the fact that the Sovereign is head of all orders of Knighthood; and the Jewelled Sword of State, symbol of honour.

The Queen was arrayed in the Royal robe and stole, which glistened with golden shamrocks, thistles and other emblems of her realm. The two great symbols of her power were then presented to her – the Sceptre with the Cross (representing royal justice and power) and the Sceptre with the Dove (representing equity and mercy). The Orb, representing independent sovereignty, was placed in her hand and the Coronation Ring, symbolizing the marriage of the monarch to her people, set upon her finger. Finally, the Archbishop raised St Edward's Crown high, bringing it down slowly to

rest on Elizabeth's head. The entire congregation cried, 'God save the Queen!'

Walking steadily, the Queen took her seat on a specially raised platform facing the high altar to receive the homage of her peers. The first to kneel before her and promise to 'become your liege man of life and limb' was the Duke of Edinburgh.

Elizabeth and Philip took Holy Communion before the congregation, then she retired to St Edward's Chapel to exchange the Crown for the lighter Imperial State Crown, and the Royal mantle for a purple velvet robe. The new Queen then emerged from the Abbey to the pealing of bells and the cheers of the jubilant crowds outside.

The new Elizabethan Age had dawned.

The Coronation tour

In the winter of 1953–4, the Queen and the Duke of Edinburgh set sail on the most momentous royal tour of all time. They visited many Commonwealth countries from prosperous Australia to remote Papua New Guinea. Elizabeth became the first reigning monarch to visit New Zealand, and the occasion was made even more historic by the fact that she broadcast her first Christmas message there.

This 'Coronation tour', as it became known, saw her opening Parliaments (wearing her Coronation dress) and greeting the peoples of Bermuda, Jamaica, Panama, Fiji, Tonga, New Zealand, Australia, the Cocos Islands, Ceylon, Aden, Uganda, Libya, Malta and Gibraltar. It was a runaway success and marked the start of her long and intimate relationship with the Commonwealth.

The tour separated Elizabeth and Philip from five-year-old Charles and three-year-old Anne for six long months. They were reunited at Gibraltar, where the children stayed with Uncle Dickie and Aunt Edwina. The Royal children were confused by the sudden appearance of their parents among flocks of officials.

♛ Ceylon left and the Cocos Islands above were just two of the Commonwealth countries visited by the new Queen and the Duke of Edinburgh during their epic tour of 1953–54. The Queen is said to have made 102 speeches in the course of the tour

♛ The births of Andrew above in 1960 and Edward right, with family four years later brought a new contentment to the Queen. The previous decade had been rather turbulent for her – now she settled down once more to the joys of motherhood and family life

🜲 *The Queen and the Duke of Edinburgh enjoyed a special relationship with Sir Winston and Lady Churchill and were frequent dinner guests at 10 Downing Street. The grand elder statesman was somewhat besotted by Queen Elizabeth – 'She's a pet,' he once said enthusiastically*

Charles even tried to shake his mother's hand – 'Not you, dear,' she said.

Once in England, life settled into the Royal routine, faithfully following its calendar – Windsor for Christmas, Sandringham for New Year, Balmoral for the summer break and Windsor for weekends. Buckingham Palace re-mained 'the shop' over which they had to live during the week, in which investitures were held and foreign dignitaries entertained. It was also the venue for the once-weekly meeting be-tween the Queen and the Prime Minister.

In 1956, there were rumours of strains on the Royal marriage as Philip set off on a solo tour of the Commonwealth on board the Royal yacht *Britannia*. He was away from his wife for four months, including their wedding anniversary and Christmas. The press seized on this as proof that the Royal marriage was 'on the rocks'. Yet the trip had been planned well in advance and Philip sent his wife a huge bouquet of white roses on their anniversary.

More Royal births

The couple were reunited at the beginning of their short Portuguese tour in February 1957. The Queen and her household greeted him wearing false beards – a joking reference to the beard he had just grown, but removed before coming to Portugal. The Duke wore a tie covered in hearts. Rumours of a rift promptly died down and in that very year the Queen created her husband a Prince of the United Kingdom.

At the grand opening of Canada's St Lawrence Seaway in June 1959, the Queen swayed dangerously and nearly fainted. Philip was at her side, deeply concerned. Elizabeth was preg-nant. Prince Andrew was born on 19 February 1960, ten years after her 'first family' had set-tled into the Palace nursery. Affairs of state had put too much pressure on the young Queen and her husband, but their longing for a larger family finally took precedence.

Just two weeks before Andrew's birth came an official change of name for the Royal Family when the Queen announced:

'Now therefore I declare my Will and Plea-sure ... while I and my children will continue to be styled and known as the House and Fami-ly of Windsor, my descendants ... shall bear the name Mountbatten-Windsor.'

The Palace added: 'The Queen has always wanted, without changing the name of the Royal House established by her grandfather, to associate the name of her husband with her own and his descendants. The Queen has had this in mind for a long time ...'

Prince Edward was born on 10 March 1964. At long last, Elizabeth and Philip had their family complete.

A REIGN REMEMBERED

The Queen's subjects have shared with her periods of happiness and sadness throughout her time as Princess and monarch. But away from the public gaze, there are a few precious mementoes that remind Elizabeth of the private moments she has spent during her childhood and, later, with Philip and their loving family

♛ The jewelled miniatures that the Queen is wearing *above* are Royal Family Orders. Pictured on the pale blue ribbon is her grandfather, George V, and on the pink, her father, George VI. The Queen also wears the famous Cambridge emeralds, inherited from Queen Mary. Some of the many presents from all over the world for Elizabeth and Philip's wedding are shown *right*

♛ Family photographs take pride of place on the Queen's desk, including *far left* an early shot of Philip – with a beard!

Rex Features

Hulton-Deutsch Collection

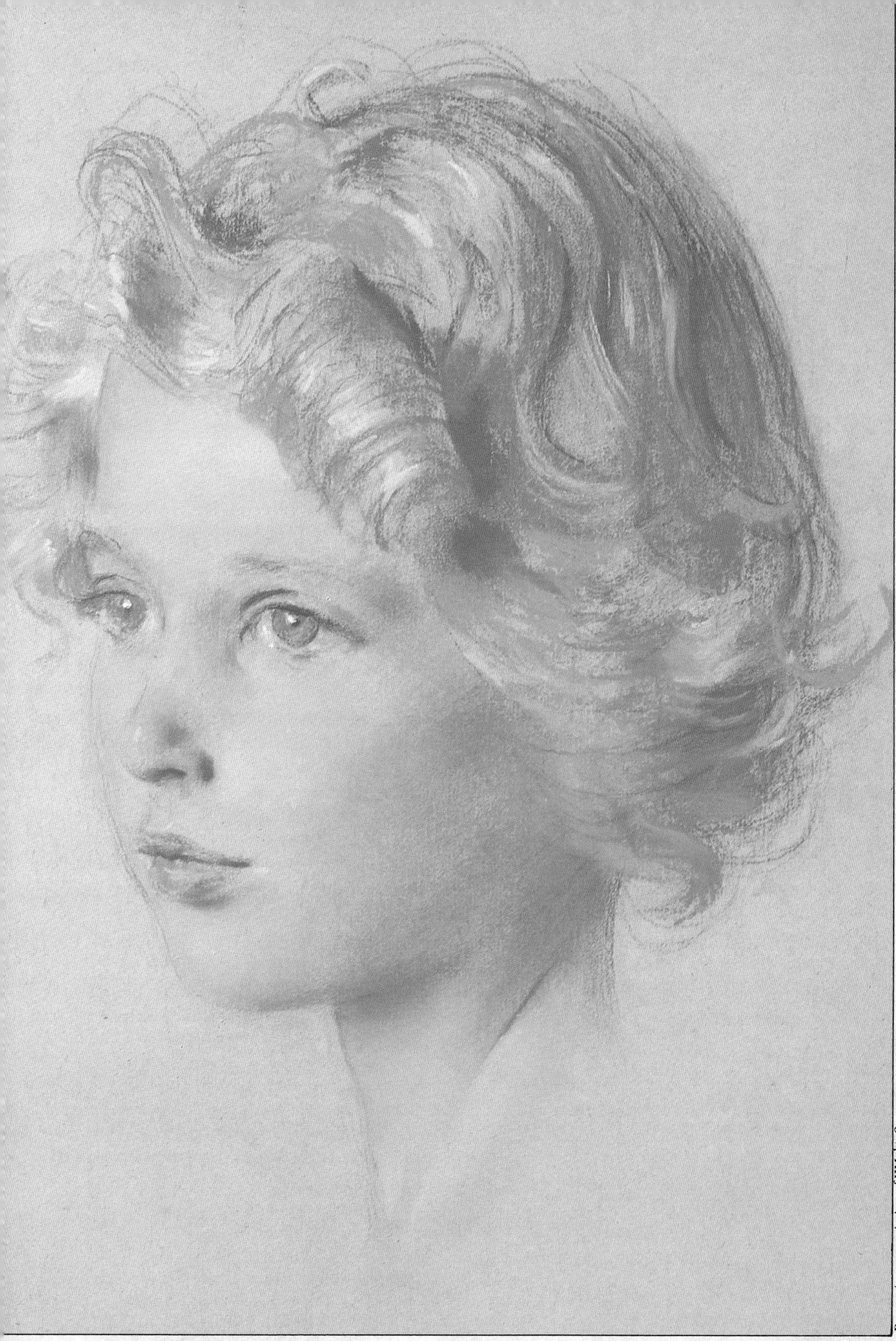

By gracious permission of HM the Queen

Marcus Adams/Camera Press

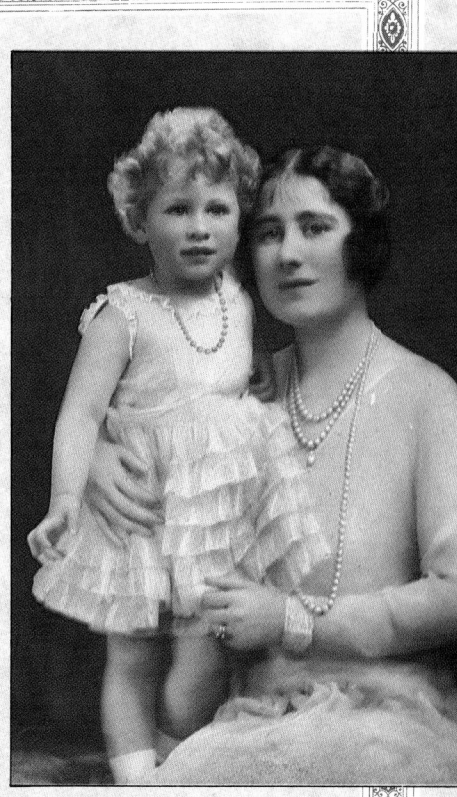

♔ **Her first piece of jewellery *above* was a delicate string of corals which are often seen in contemporary pictures. The necklace belonged to her mother at a similar age. Elizabeth, in turn, passed it on to her own daughter, Princess Anne**

♔ **At Christmas 1943, 17-year-old Elizabeth starred as Aladdin in Windsor Castle's own pantomime *below*, but few people could guess that Philip Mountbatten, who was in the audience, was to be her future leading man**

♔ **A fleeting moment of childhood is beautifully caught in this cherished portrait of seven-year-old Princess Anne *above* by A K Lawrence. It shows a remarkable resemblance to her mother as a little girl**

♔ **A teddy for baby Elizabeth to prize *left*. It was given to her by her mother shortly after her birth**

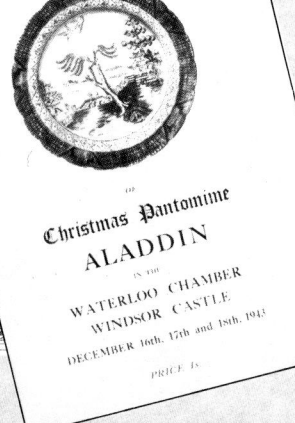

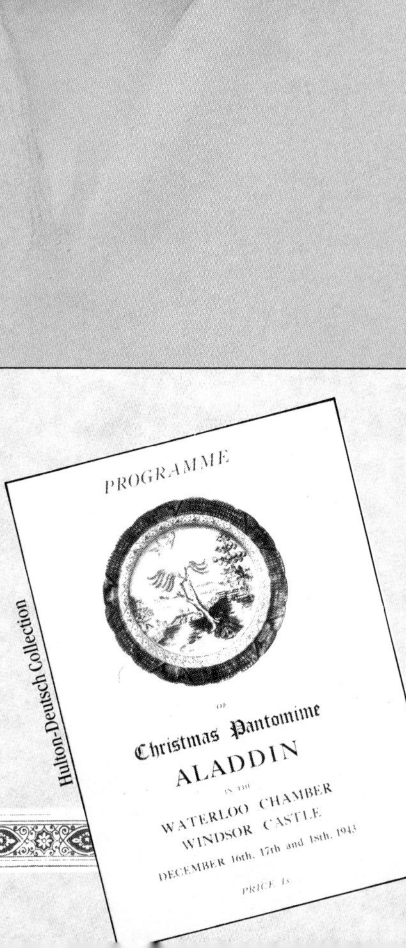
PROGRAMME
OF
Christmas Pantomime
ALADDIN
IN THE
WATERLOO CHAMBER
WINDSOR CASTLE
DECEMBER 16th, 17th and 18th, 1943
PRICE 1s.

Hulton-Deutsch Collection

Popperfoto

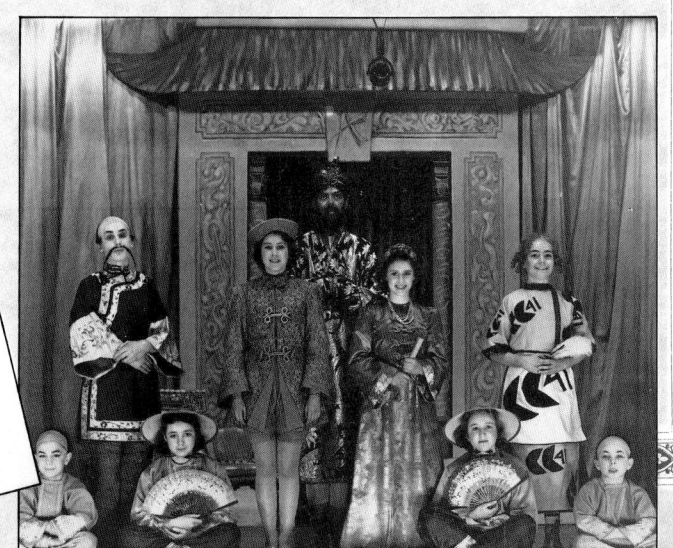

Karsh/Camera Press

MONARCH FOR A MODERN AGE

THE QUEEN AND PRINCE PHILIP HAVE HAD TO COPE WITH EVER-INCREASING MEDIA INTEREST, YET THE STRENGTH OF THEIR RELATIONSHIP HAS ENABLED THEM TO PRESERVE THE MONARCHY AS BRITAIN'S BEST-LOVED INSTITUTION

IN RESPONSE TO A PERFECTLY POLITE QUESTION, 'How was your flight, Sir?' Philip once replied, 'Have you ever flown? Well, like that.' Acerbic, witty and unpredictable, Philip has managed to annoy almost every section of society, but, paradoxically, he is also widely admired.

By anyone's standards, his has not been an easy marriage. It does not come readily to one of his character to walk a few paces behind his wife or to adjust to life ' in the royal goldfish bowl'.

His main problem lies in his complete lack of a clear-cut role. 'Constitutionally I don't exist,' he admits ruefully. Like Victoria's Prince Consort, however, he has found a wealth of interests, many of them serious, such as the World Wildlife Fund for which he works tirelessly. He also takes a personal interest in communications to the Palace and his secretaries have been briefed to pass on to him letters that would be of particular interest.

When he chooses, he can be self-deprecatory about his 'coming second'. At an official function, he was introduced to a 'Dr and Mr Robinson'. The gentleman in question explained: 'In our family, my wife comes first.' 'Yes,' replied Philip, 'we have that problem in our family too.' And in 1965, he addressed a dinner given by the Welsh Guards, 'What is unique about this regiment? I will tell you. It is the only one in which the Colonel is legally married to the Colonel-in-Chief.'

Inevitably, there have been strains on the marriage. Some days are icy, and Royal rows are not unknown. Nevertheless, he is the Queen's staunchest champion and supporter, whether it is her dignity or her person that is threatened. A typical example of this was during a Silver Jubilee walkabout in Glasgow, in 1977, when she was suddenly engulfed by thousands of hysterical children. The police tried to carve a path to rescue her – but a concerned Philip was at her side first.

The head of the family

Philip is very much the head of the family and the Queen trusts his judgement implicitly in family matters. 'I'll ask Papa,' is her stand-by answer to difficult decisions within their close circle. But on matters of State – particularly where the Commonwealth is concerned – she is resolutely Head and does not mince her words if she feels her outspoken consort has stepped out of line.

One matter on which the couple will never see eye-to-eye is Philip's long-standing friendship with Hélène Cordet. During his engagement he continued their friendship although Palace staff tried to warn him off. In this, as in everything else, however, he is his own man. Philip is still happy to continue the friendship, actively taking an interest in her son's education; Max, Philip's godson, went to school at Gor-

👑 *Balmoral Castle in the northeast of Scotland has always been a favourite holiday retreat of the Queen and Prince Philip. If it is possible, every autumn they gather there with their family around them*

Hulton-Deutsch Collection

Hulton-Deutsch Collection

donstoun before going on to Cambridge.

Philip's relationship with Elizabeth is primarily based on laughter. One shared joke involves the Biblical quote: 'weeping and wailing and gnashing of teeth'. No one knows what it means to them, but just hearing those words can cause the Queen to dissolve into hoots of laughter.

In 1972, Elizabeth and Philip celebrated their Silver Wedding, with a Thanksgiving Service at St Paul's Cathedral, a luncheon at the Guildhall and a walkabout. The Queen said to the august company, 'I think everyone will concede that today, of all occasions, I should begin my speech with "My husband and I".' After the laughter had died down, she went on to quote a bishop who, when asked what he thought about sin, replied, 'I am against it.' If she were asked what she thought of family life she said she would answer, 'I am for it.'

Charles and Anne

From the very start, Elizabeth and Philip have been determined that their children should mix with as many other young people as possible. Charles attended both his father's old schools – Cheam Preparatory School in Surrey and Gordonstoun, where, although he eventually became 'Guardian', he was never happy. His first weeks there were punctuated with secret telephone calls to 'Granny' who was sympathetic, but counselled soldiering on.

Then followed a course at Trinity College, Cambridge, where Charles gained a respectable degree in Archaeology and Anthropology, with a term at the University College of Wales to study the Welsh language under the tutelage of a Welsh nationalist. Never entirely happy with his peers, he did mix, taking part in college theatricals.

The Queen was always unsure about what to do with Anne. Mother and daughter have

♛ *The Queen's enduring reign and obviously happy marriage to Prince Philip has been a source of envy to other royal families. As the interest in them becomes almost insatiable, and their workload increases, the admiration of their subjects remains steadfast*

A WEEKLY RENDEZVOUS

Hulton-Deutsch Collection

The weekly meeting between the Queen and her Prime Minister every Tuesday is a great British tradition. In her 36-year reign, the Queen has dealt with eight Prime Ministers – Sir Winston Churchill, Sir Anthony Eden, Sir Harold Macmillan, Sir Alec Douglas-Home, Sir Harold Wilson, Edward Heath, Sir James Callaghan and Margaret Thatcher. Contrary to what some people believe, she does not automatically favour Tory Prime Ministers. Harold Wilson *left* and James Callaghan were both particular Royal favourites, enjoying many a joke with the Queen. Relations with the present Prime Minister, Margaret Thatcher, are rumoured to be less cordial

John Shelley

John Shelley

THE COMMONWEALTH OF NATIONS

During her years as Queen, Elizabeth has made the Commonwealth her special area of interest. The advent of jet travel has meant that she has been able to visit far more countries than any of her predecessors. Even the tiny Tuvalu islands, north of Fiji (shown *above* in an October 1982 visit), have not been overlooked. Concerned with the problems of her 'global family', she has maintained contact with many ex-Empire nations, which have long gained independence, such as India. Her relationship with the late Indira Gandhi (pictured *left* on Elizabeth's visit in November 1983) was particularly valued

always had an explosive relationship and, when Anne hankered after being sent away to school, it may well have seemed the best solution. The first thing that the Princess noticed about Benenden in Kent was 'the deafening noise'. On the whole, she had a happy adolescence, making friends and pursuing her increasingly important hobby, riding.

After schooldays in the footsteps of his father, Charles pursued a career that also emulated Philip's – learning to fly with the RAF at Cranwell, then into the Navy for five years, ending with the command of his own ship, HMS *Bronnington*, in 1976. From then on, training to be King was to become his career, while Anne developed her considerable talents

as a three-day-eventer, becoming European Champion and the BBC Sports Personality of the Year in 1971, perhaps fulfilling her mother's own secret ambition. Had she not been Queen, Elizabeth could well have been a first-class rider; certainly Anne's success helped endear her to her mother and smooth over the pricklier patches in their previously stormy relationship.

The second family

In the ten years between their two 'families', Elizabeth and Philip had learned a great deal about bringing up children in the limelight. They did not want Andrew or Edward to suffer the same media attention as Charles and Anne,

👑 *One of the Queen's proudest moments was the Investiture of her son Charles as the Prince of Wales. She presented him to the people at Caernarvon Castle on 1 July 1969. He wore a specially designed coronet made of Welsh gold*

but were, nevertheless, insistent that their younger children had similar upbringings.

After nursery lessons at the Palace, which he shared with aristocratic friends and cousin Viscount Linley, Andrew was packed off to the preparatory school at Heatherdown near Windsor.

Then came the inevitable Gordonstoun, which Andrew found much more congenial than had his sensitive elder brother.

He did well at school, especially in the Gordonstoun Air Training Corps where he shone, earning his pilot's wings at the age of 16, and he gained six 'O' levels.

The dashing young pilot

The next two years were spent at Lakesfield in Canada, at the suggestion of Prime Minister Pierre Trudeau. By now he had discovered girls – and they flocked to discover him. But he had to take his 'A' levels and round off his education back home. He left Gordonstoun in 1978, gaining respectable passes in English, Political Studies and History, and almost immediately began his career as a Royal Navy pilot. In 1982 his courage was to be tested in the Falklands conflict, while acting as a decoy for Exocet missiles or air-lifting the wounded from stormy seas to base.

Andrew is said to be the Queen's favourite child, and it is not difficult to imagine how she must have felt during those worrying times.

Meanwhile, Edward was growing up under the protective wings of the 'first family'.

Charles spent time telling him stories (one of which was published under the title *The Old Man of Lochnagar*) and trying to teach him about music. Anne was unusually sympathetic towards her last brother, although she tended to hide her feelings under a gruff exterior.

Edward followed Andrew's footsteps – to Heatherdown in 1972, then on to Gordonstoun, where he outshone both his brothers academically, gaining nine 'O' levels and good 'A' level passes in English, Politics and Economics, and History. He gained his gliding wings in 1980 and in 1982 won his private pilot's licence.

His Commonwealth education was gained as a junior master at Wanganui Collegiate School in New Zealand in 1982, followed immediately by his entering Jesus College, Cambridge, to read Archaeology and Anthropology in which he graduated in 1986. While at Cambridge, he became an enthusiastic amateur actor, an interest that has developed since.

A family crisis

When life as a trainee Royal Marine proved not to be to his cup of tea, Edward took the courageous step of admitting it and resigning. Tempers at the Palace – expecially his father's – were said to flare, and adroitly, perhaps, he made amends by 'fronting' the Duke of Edinburgh's Award Scheme, besides becoming patron of theatrical charities and organizations. Edward's keen interest in theatricals made him organize the other younger Royals in a TV game show for charity in 1987, and in 1988 he began work as Production Assistant with Andrew Lloyd Webber's Really Useful Theatre Company – making him the first of the Queen's children to earn a salary from a private enterprise.

♛ *Philip's most enjoyable leisure interest has been four-in-hand carriage driving. He has entered – and succeeded in winning – many competitions. One event he particularly cherishes winning is the 1982 Carriage Driving Grand Prix at the Windsor Horse Show*

♛ *The Queen and Prince Philip share a mutual love of horses – a love they have passed on to most of their children. Although the Prince plays polo less than he used to, he likes to umpire matches when he can and, if time permits, the Queen loves to join him*

Tim Graham

👑 *The Trooping of the Colour ceremony has been an annual event in June since 1805. Throughout her reign, the Queen has led her troops as Commander-in-Chief of the armed forces down Horse Guards' Parade and along the Mall. She is seen* above *leaving Buckingham Palace*

Wales's Investiture at Caernarvon Castle. Both of these events were milestones in their way; the television spectacle took a year to make, with cameras following the Royal Family on both public and private business. Now, for the first time ever, the public were to see informal shots of the Queen chatting with her family around the breakfast table, at parties, talking to ambassadors, and generally relaxing and joking with her children. The programme was a roaring success and changed the image of the British Royals immeasurably for the better.

A new Prince of Wales

The Investiture of Charles as Prince of Wales was fraught with danger and required months of planning. Welsh nationalists threatened his life; a number of bombs did go off on the day, but fortunately no one was hurt. The talents of Lord Snowdon, Keeper of Caernarvon Castle, were used to enhance the image of the ceremony; inevitably there were criticisms. The transparent awning he had designed drew comments about 'pomp and perspex' but he persuaded his sister-in-law to wear a modern version of a medieval hat, laced with pearls, which won popular approval. It was Charles' day; his sincerity was almost painful to watch and the love between mother and son as the Queen presented him to the Welsh people was deeply moving.

Another Royal Family

The year 1973 saw the marriage of Anne and Captain Mark Phillips, a love match that delighted the Royal Family. The subsequent births of Peter, born in Jubilee Year (1977), and Zara (born in 1981) enabled the Queen, for the first time, to show her considerable talents as a grandmother; firm, but with endless patience and often bursting with fun. (She was to use these talents again later, with the births of Charles and Diana's sons – William, in 1982, and Harry in 1984.) Anne herself was soon to emerge as a forthright woman with a mission, earning enormous respect as President of the Save the Children Fund and patron of Riding for the Disabled. In 1987 she finally accepted the Queen's offer of the title Princess Royal in recognition of her untiring work for the sick and underprivileged.

Royal pressures

Anne was the first to suffer from a series of dangerous incidents that were to plague the Royal Family. Driving back from an official function in 1974, a gunman stopped them in the Mall, shooting the chauffeur and her bodyguard and attempting to kidnap the Princess. Passers-by chased the man off. Hysterical and shocked, the Princess chose to talk to her father – always her closest ally – over the phone (her

Modern royalty must, however grudgingly, accommodate the growing demands of the media. The Queen's Christmas message and photographs of the Royal Family in newspapers and magazines were the limit of this sort of cooperation when the Queen came to the throne. But 1969 was to see the showing of *The Royal Family* film made by the BBC, and the Prince of

parents were away from home at the time).

In 1979, the world was shocked to hear of the death of Lord Mountbatten, the Royal Family's beloved 'Uncle Dickie', who was murdered in Ireland by the IRA. At his State funeral in Westminster Abbey, Prince Charles said in his address, 'I still cannot believe that I am standing here delivering an address about a man who, to me, always seemed reassuringly indestructible.' After a more private service at Romsey Abbey, Charles broke down and cried. Philip, whose life had been so thoroughly charted by his uncle, was granite-faced with pent-up grief.

Danger threatened the Queen herself in 1981, when a demented 17-year-old fired blank shots at her as she rode to the Trooping of the Colour. Although she said later that her concern was for 'those behind me' – her husband and son – her royal reflexes were such that she did not look round, but carried on with the ceremony. In 1982, the Queen woke to find that a strange man, Michael Fagan, had broken into the Palace and was standing beside her bed dripping blood from a self-inflicted wound. It is a measure of her courage that she calmly managed to keep the deluded intruder talking until finally the police arrived.

'I pledged my life to the service of our people'

QUEEN ELIZABETH ON HER SILVER JUBILEE

The Queen's Silver Jubilee in 1977 reaffirmed the magic of the monarchy. Suddenly, the nation came alive as everyone was united in a glittering celebration of her 25 years of reign. Walkabouts were to be a main feature of the celebrations – the most memorable being her walk through the City of London on Silver Jubilee Day. Thousands of people turned out to greet her, wearing silver decorations and funny hats and carrying Union Jacks. The surge of warmth and emotion was overwhelming – a true private bond between a monarch and her people. It was a grey day, but the Queen glowed in pink. As always, Philip was to be a few paces behind, dressed in the uniform of an Admiral of the Fleet, joking with the crowds, and generally offering moral support. In a Silver Jubilee speech the Queen reminded the nation of her promise made six years before her Coronation. 'When I was 21, I pledged my life to the service of our people and I asked for God's help to make good that vow . . . I do not regret or retract one word of it.'

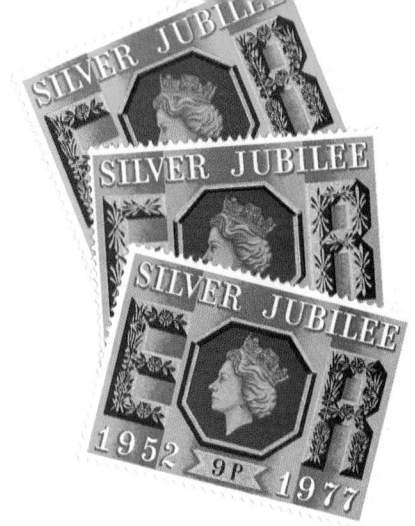

June 1977 saw the Queen and Prince Philip celebrate 25 years of her reign in St Paul's Cathedral. The whole nation joined in with street parties and firework displays

Photographers International

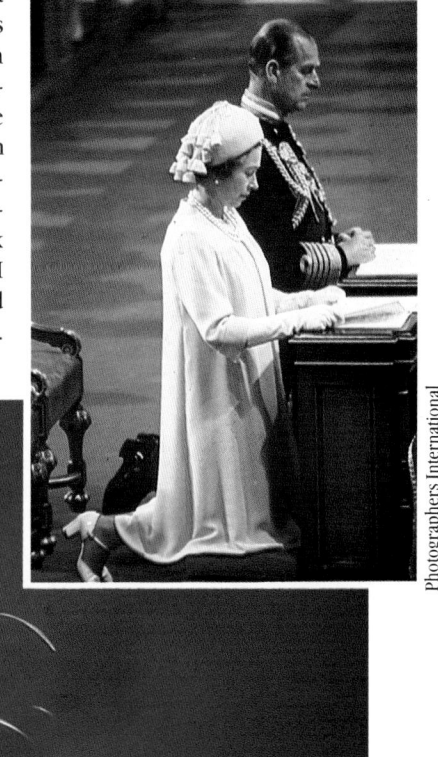

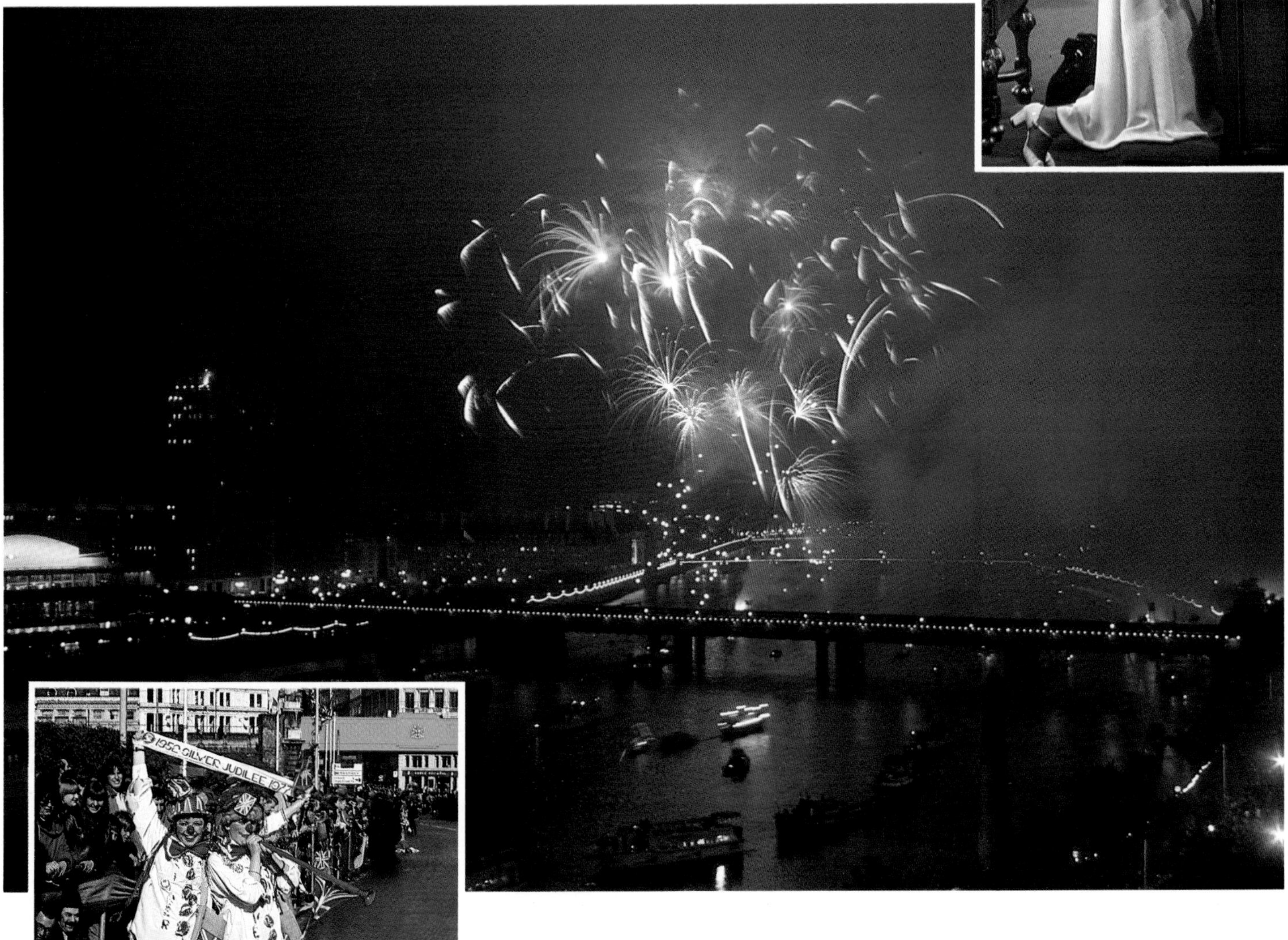

Camera Press

Photographers International

Patrick Lichfield/Camera Press

FORTY YEARS TOGETHER

The wedding of Charles in 1981 created a new Royal superstar in Diana – the 'girl next door' who worked in a kindergarten and captured the nation's heart. Elizabeth and Philip's pleasure was plain to see. At the Royal party held in honour of the young bride and groom, Philip wore a 'Charles and Diana' boater and the Queen danced to a steel band.

Undoubtedly the Queen's happiest day, however, was the wedding of Andrew and Sarah Ferguson in 1986. By the time of the marriage, 'Fergie' was already a Royal favourite, being intelligent, energetic, independent and fun.

Her determination to continue her work for a publisher of fine art books earned her admiration from the Queen, who put an office at Buckingham Palace at her disposal. Even allowing herself to be filmed in her underslip, trying on clothes, was viewed tolerantly by Elizabeth, whose attitude to fashion is similar to Sarah's. 'I like to keep busy,' Sarah told David Frost in 1987, 'I don't sit around worrying about what to wear the next day.'

The celebration of the Queen's sixtieth birthday in 1986 saw a much more relaxed monarch (with Sarah firmly at her side), than at any previous grand occasion. She realized that she no longer had any real critics. This lady, with her corgis, her headscarves and her one passionate hobby, flat racing, had earned her place in the affections of millions the world over. ITN journalist Trevor Macdonald, who made a documentary about the Queen and Commonwealth in 1986, said, 'One tends to take the Queen for granted. But the most amazing thing I found is the esteem in which she's held throughout the Commonwealth. She is universally *adored*.'

Ruby wedding

Today, Elizabeth has one of the busiest schedules in the world. Her programme is planned a year in advance and, apart from her many State visits and Royal functions, she still handles over 200 letters a day. Although she is the sole monarch, there is no doubt that one of her greatest strengths has been the support of the man she loves – who has always been there to offer help and encouragement whenever needed. And with the birth of their fifth grandchild Princess Beatrice, in 1988, the happiness they have shared together for over forty years will hopefully continue for many more.

👑 *Four generations of royalty joined the Queen and Philip to celebrate the christening of their fourth grandchild, Prince Harry, in 1984*

Snowdon/Camera Press